Keras & Deep Learning
100 Interview Questions

X.Y. Wang

Contents

1 Introduction   **5**

2 Basic   **7**

  2.1   What is Keras, and what are its main features? . . .   7

  2.2   Can you explain the difference between Keras and TensorFlow? 8

  2.3   What are the main components of a neural network in Keras? 9

  2.4   What are the different types of layers in Keras, and what are their purposes? 10

  2.5   How do you initialize a Sequential model in Keras, and what is its purpose? 12

  2.6   What is the role of activation functions in a neural network, and can you name a few common activation functions used in Keras? 13

  2.7   How do you compile a Keras model, and what are the key parameters required? 14

  2.8   What is the purpose of the fit() function in Keras, and what are some important parameters to consider when using it? 15

2.9   Can you explain the role of optimizers in Keras, and
       provide examples of some commonly used optimizers?   16

2.10   What is the difference between overfitting and under-
       fitting in deep learning, and how can you prevent them
       in a Keras model?   17

2.11   What are loss functions, and why are they important
       in Keras? Can you provide examples of some com-
       monly used loss functions?   19

2.12   What is the purpose of the evaluate() function in
       Keras, and what information does it provide?   20

2.13   How do you use the predict() function in Keras, and
       what does it return?   21

2.14   What is the role of batch size in training a Keras
       model, and how does it affect model performance? . .   22

2.15   How do you save and load a trained Keras model? . .   23

2.16   What is the purpose of using callbacks in Keras, and
       can you provide examples of some commonly used call-
       backs?   24

2.17   What are the differences between the Keras functional
       API and the Sequential model?   25

2.18   How do you apply regularization techniques in Keras,
       such as L1 and L2 regularization?   26

2.19   Can you explain the concept of early stopping in Keras,
       and how it helps prevent overfitting?   28

2.20   What is transfer learning, and how can you implement
       it using Keras?   29

3 Intermediate   31

3.1   What is the difference between a Dense layer and a
       Convolutional layer in Keras, and when would you use
       each?   31

3.2 Can you explain the concept of recurrent neural networks (RNNs) and how they can be implemented in Keras? 32

3.3 What is the purpose of dropout layers in Keras, and how do they help prevent overfitting? 33

3.4 How do you handle imbalanced datasets in Keras, and what techniques can you use to address this issue? . . 34

3.5 What are the advantages of using batch normalization in Keras, and how do you implement it in a model? . . 36

3.6 Can you explain the concept of gradient clipping in Keras, and why it might be useful during training? . . 37

3.7 How do you handle missing or corrupted data when preparing a dataset for a Keras model? 38

3.8 What is the purpose of an embedding layer in Keras, and when would you use one? 40

3.9 How do you perform hyperparameter tuning in Keras to optimize the performance of a model? 41

3.10 Can you explain the concept of a 1D, 2D, and 3D convolution in Keras, and provide an example of when each might be used? 44

3.11 How do you use pre-trained word embeddings, such as Word2Vec or GloVe, in a Keras model? 45

3.12 What is the purpose of a custom layer in Keras, and how do you create one? 48

3.13 How do you perform cross-validation in Keras to assess the performance of your model? 49

3.14 What is the purpose of a generator in Keras, and how can you create a custom generator for your dataset? . 50

3.15 How do you implement multi-output or multi-input models in Keras using the functional API? 52

3.16   Can you explain the concept of a residual connection, and how it can be implemented in Keras?   53

3.17   What are the differences between stateful and stateless RNNs in Keras, and when should you use each?   55

3.18   How do you visualize the architecture and training progress of a Keras model?   56

3.19   What are some strategies for handling overfitting and underfitting when using convolutional neural networks (CNNs) in Keras?   57

3.20   Can you explain the difference between one-shot learning and few-shot learning, and how Keras can be used for these tasks?   58

4   Advanced   **61**

4.1   Can you explain the concept of attention mechanisms in neural networks, and how they can be implemented in Keras?   61

4.2   What are the key differences between GRU and LSTM layers in Keras, and when might you choose one over the other?   62

4.3   How do you implement custom loss functions and custom metrics in Keras, and when would you need to do so?   64

4.4   Can you describe the process of creating an end-to-end pipeline for a deep learning project using Keras? . . .   65

4.5   What are some advanced techniques for data augmentation in Keras, and how do they help improve model performance?   67

4.6   How do you parallelize the training of a Keras model using multiple GPUs, and what are the main challenges involved?   68

4.7   What is the role of skip connections in neural net-
       works, and how do you implement them using the Keras
       functional API?   70

4.8   Can you explain the concept of teacher forcing in
       sequence-to-sequence models, and how it can be im-
       plemented in Keras?   71

4.9   How do you deal with variable-length input sequences
       in Keras, particularly in the context of RNNs?   73

4.10   What is the purpose of using reinforcement learning
       with Keras, and how can you implement it?   75

4.11   How do you fine-tune a pre-trained Keras model, and
       what are some best practices to consider during this
       process?   76

4.12   Can you explain the concept of adversarial training
       and how it can be used with Keras to improve model
       robustness?   78

4.13   What are some key differences between autoencoders
       and variational autoencoders, and how can they be im-
       plemented in Keras?   79

4.14   How do you perform model ensembling in Keras, and
       what are the advantages of this approach?   81

4.15   What is the purpose of using Keras with a distributed
       training framework like Horovod or TensorFlow's tf.dis-
       tribute?   83

4.16   Can you explain the concept of curriculum learning,
       and how it can be applied in a Keras model?   84

4.17   How do you implement custom training loops in Keras,
       and when would you need to do so?   85

4.18   What are some best practices for managing memory
       usage and optimizing performance when training large-
       scale models in Keras?   87

4.19 How do you use Keras to perform transfer learning across different modalities, such as images and text? . 88

4.20 Can you explain the concept of learning rate scheduling in Keras, and how it can be used to improve model convergence? 90

5 Expert **93**

5.1 Can you explain the concept of neural architecture search (NAS), and how it can be applied using Keras? 93

5.2 How do you implement multi-task learning in Keras, and what are the main challenges involved? 95

5.3 What is the purpose of using a Bayesian optimization approach for hyperparameter tuning in Keras, and how can you implement it? 97

5.4 Can you explain the concept of knowledge distillation, and how it can be used in Keras to create smaller, more efficient models? 98

5.5 How do you implement unsupervised and self-supervised learning techniques using Keras, and what are their main advantages? 100

5.6 What are some advanced techniques for visualizing the learned features and decision-making processes of a Keras model? 102

5.7 How do you handle out-of-vocabulary (OOV) tokens when working with text data in Keras, and what are some best practices for doing so? 104

5.8 Can you explain the concept of continual learning, and how it can be implemented in Keras to allow models to adapt to new data over time? 105

5.9 What are the main challenges of scaling Keras models to work with large datasets, and what are some techniques to overcome these challenges? 107

5.10 How do you use Keras to perform multi-modal learn-
      ing, where the model must process and integrate data
      from multiple sources or modalities? 108

5.11 Can you explain the concept of meta-learning, and
      how it can be applied using Keras to learn new tasks
      more quickly? 110

5.12 What are some techniques for improving the inter-
      pretability and explainability of deep learning models
      in Keras? 111

5.13 How do you use Keras to perform zero-shot or few-shot
      learning, where models must generalize to new classes
      without seeing any labeled examples? 112

5.14 Can you explain the concept of graph neural networks
      (GNNs) and how they can be implemented using Keras? 114

5.15 How do you design and implement custom activation
      functions, and what are some considerations when do-
      ing so in Keras? 115

5.16 What are some techniques for optimizing the deploy-
      ment of Keras models on edge devices or mobile plat-
      forms? 117

5.17 How do you implement active learning in Keras to ef-
      fectively select samples for labeling and improve model
      performance with less labeled data? 118

5.18 Can you explain the concept of capsule networks, and
      how they can be implemented in Keras to improve
      model robustness and generalization? 119

5.19 What are some best practices for managing the lifecy-
      cle of a Keras model, from development to deployment
      and maintenance? 121

5.20 How do you evaluate the fairness and ethical consider-
      ations of a Keras model, and what are some techniques
      to mitigate potential biases in model predictions? . . . 123

6   Guru   125

6.1   Can you discuss the challenges and limitations of the
      current Keras API in the context of emerging deep
      learning research trends and new architectures? 125

6.2   What are some key considerations for designing and
      implementing custom training algorithms in Keras that
      efficiently leverage the underlying hardware capabilities?126

6.3   How do you adapt Keras to leverage emerging hard-
      ware architectures, such as neuromorphic computing or
      quantum computing platforms, for deep learning tasks? 128

6.4   Can you explain the trade-offs involved in designing a
      scalable and maintainable deep learning system archi-
      tecture that combines Keras with other components,
      such as data processing pipelines and model serving
      infrastructure? 130

6.5   How can Keras be integrated with other machine learn-
      ing frameworks or libraries to enable more effective
      multi-framework workflows and facilitate collaboration
      across different research communities? 131

6.6   Can you discuss the role of Keras in the development
      and standardization of new deep learning and machine
      learning benchmarks, as well as the evaluation of new
      model architectures and training techniques? 132

6.7   What are some key challenges in developing a more
      unified and extensible Keras API that can support a
      broader range of deep learning tasks, including unsu-
      pervised, self-supervised, and reinforcement learning? . 133

6.8   How can Keras be adapted to support more advanced
      optimization techniques, such as second-order optimiza-
      tion methods, that may offer improved convergence
      properties and better generalization performance? . . 135

6.9 What are some key considerations when implementing privacy-preserving techniques, such as federated learning or differential privacy, in Keras to ensure that models can be trained and deployed in sensitive or regulated environments? 138

6.10 Can you discuss the role of Keras in enabling more effective collaboration between the deep learning research community and other scientific disciplines, such as neuroscience, cognitive science, and psychology, to advance our understanding of learning and intelligence? 140

6.11 How can Keras be used to support research on the integration of symbolic reasoning and deep learning, enabling more powerful and interpretable models that can perform complex reasoning tasks? 141

6.12 What are some key challenges and best practices for developing and maintaining a large-scale, production-ready Keras codebase that can support the rapid iteration and deployment of new deep learning models and features? 143

6.13 How can Keras be extended to support emerging research areas, such as learning with less data, transfer learning across domains or tasks, or learning in adversarial environments, where traditional deep learning approaches may struggle? 145

6.14 What are some key considerations for adapting Keras to support more advanced model architectures and learning paradigms, such as dynamic computation graphs, differentiable programming, or neuro-symbolic architectures? 146

6.15 Can you discuss the role of Keras in advancing the state of the art in deep learning-based natural language processing, computer vision, and other application domains, as well as the key challenges and opportunities in these areas? 148

6.16 How can Keras be used to develop more robust and re-
      liable deep learning models that can effectively handle
      uncertainty, noise, or distribution shifts in the input
      data, or that can be more easily verified and validated? 149

6.17 What are some key challenges and opportunities in us-
      ing Keras to develop more energy-efficient deep learn-
      ing models and training algorithms that can help ad-
      dress the growing computational and environmental
      costs of deep learning research and deployment? 151

6.18 How can Keras support research on more biologically
      plausible deep learning models and learning algorithms
      that can shed light on the neural mechanisms under-
      lying learning and cognition, and potentially lead to
      more powerful and efficient artificial systems? 153

6.19 Can you discuss the role of Keras in the development
      and evaluation of novel deep learning-based approaches
      to unsolved or open-ended problems, such as artificial
      general intelligence, common sense reasoning, or cre-
      ativity? 154

6.20 What are some key considerations for developing and
      maintaining a thriving open-source ecosystem around
      Keras, including fostering collaboration, ensuring re-
      producibility, and promoting the responsible and ethi-
      cal use of deep learning technologies? 156

Chapter 1

Introduction

The field of deep learning has witnessed unprecedented growth and progress over the past decade. The ability to automatically learn and extract high-level features from raw data has made deep learning a cornerstone technology for a wide range of applications, from computer vision and natural language processing to speech recognition and reinforcement learning. As a result, the demand for skilled deep learning practitioners has soared, and understanding the intricacies of deep learning frameworks and architectures has become a vital skill in the job market.

Keras, an open-source deep learning library, has emerged as one of the most popular and user-friendly tools for building, training, and deploying deep learning models. With its high-level, intuitive API and support for multiple backends such as TensorFlow, Microsoft Cognitive Toolkit, and Theano, Keras has become the go-to library for researchers and practitioners alike.

"Keras and Deep Learning: 100 Interview Questions" is a comprehensive guide designed to help you navigate the complexities of Keras and deep learning. It offers a structured approach to learning by categorizing questions into four difficulty levels—Basic, Intermediate, Advanced, and Expert—ensuring a smooth progression as you build your understanding of Keras and its applications in deep learning.

This book covers a wide range of topics, from fundamental concepts and components of neural networks in Keras to advanced techniques such as neural architecture search, meta-learning, and active learning. You'll explore questions related to various aspects of deep learning, including model training and evaluation, hyperparameter tuning, regularization techniques, data augmentation, transfer learning, and more. Additionally, you'll delve into specific architectures, such as recurrent neural networks, convolutional neural networks, and graph neural networks, along with their applications and nuances.

Whether you are preparing for a job interview, looking to enhance your knowledge, or simply seeking to gain insights into the world of Keras and deep learning, this book is your one-stop resource. With detailed explanations, examples, and practical advice, "Keras and Deep Learning: 100 Interview Questions" equips you with the knowledge and confidence you need to excel in your deep learning endeavors and achieve success in your professional pursuits.

Chapter 2

Basic

2.1 What is Keras, and what are its main features?

Keras is an open-source deep learning framework written in Python. It is designed to provide a user-friendly interface for building and training deep neural networks. Keras allows researchers and developers to build complex models quickly and easily, without having to write a lot of boilerplate code. Some of the main features of Keras include:

1. User friendliness: Keras is designed to be easy to use, with a simple and intuitive API that can be used by beginners and experts alike. This makes it possible to build complex deep learning models quickly and easily, without having to write a lot of code.

2. Modular and composable: Keras is built on a modular architecture that allows researchers and developers to mix and match different layers, loss functions, and optimization algorithms to create new models. This makes it easy to experiment with different architectures and to reuse code.

3. GPU and TPU acceleration: Keras supports GPU and TPU acceleration, which allows deep learning models to be trained much faster

than on a CPU.

4. Extensibility: Keras is highly extensible, with a large user community that develops new layers, loss functions, and optimization algorithms.

5. Built-in support for various types of data: Keras can handle a wide variety of data, including images, text, and time series data. It also provides preprocessing functions for data normalization, augmentation, and other tasks.

6. Compatibility: Keras is compatible with a wide variety of back-end deep learning engines, including TensorFlow, Microsoft Cognitive Toolkit, Theano, and CNTK. This means that Keras models can be run on a variety of hardware platforms, including CPUs, GPUs, and TPUs.

Overall, Keras is a powerful and flexible deep learning framework that provides a user-friendly interface for building and training deep neural networks. Its modular design, GPU and TPU acceleration, and built-in support for various types of data make it a popular choice for researchers and developers in the field of deep learning.

2.2 Can you explain the difference between Keras and TensorFlow?

Keras and TensorFlow are both deep learning frameworks that are widely used in the machine learning community. They have a lot of overlapping functionality but they also have some differences.

TensorFlow is an open-source deep learning framework developed by Google. It provides a low-level API for building and training machine learning models. This means that TensorFlow gives users a lot of control over the model architecture and optimization process. TensorFlow has a lot of advanced features such as distributed computing, which can be used to scale up the training process to multiple GPUs, and automatic differentiation, which can be used to calculate gradients automatically.

Keras, on the other hand, is a high-level API developed by Francois

Chollet. It is built on top of TensorFlow, Theano, or CNTK. Keras is designed to be user-friendly and easy to use, which makes it a popular choice for beginners in machine learning. Keras provides a simplified interface for building and training deep learning models. This means that users do not need to have a deep understanding of the low-level details of the model architecture or the optimization process.

One of the major differences between Keras and TensorFlow is the level of abstraction they provide. TensorFlow provides a lower-level API that gives users more control over the model architecture and optimization process, but this also means that it can be more challenging to use. Keras, on the other hand, provides a higher-level API that is easier to use but does not offer as much flexibility.

Another difference between Keras and TensorFlow is the number of pre-built models and layers available. TensorFlow has a larger collection of pre-built models and layers, while Keras provides a smaller, but still significant, set of these.

In summary, TensorFlow is a low-level API designed for users who have a deep understanding of deep learning models, architecture, and optimization. Keras is a higher-level API designed for users who want to quickly build and train deep learning models without a lot of knowledge of the underlying details.

2.3   What are the main components of a neural network in Keras?

In Keras, a neural network is composed of different types of layers, each serving a specific purpose. The main layers in a typical neural network include:

1. **Input Layer**: This layer specifies the input shape of the data that will be fed to the network. It's the first layer in the network and is responsible for accepting the input data.

2. **Hidden Layers**: These are the layers between the input and output layer where most of the computations occur. They consist of multiple layers of neurons, each processing input data in a particular

way by applying a non-linear activation function.

3. **Output Layer**: This layer produces the final output of the neural network. The number of neurons in the output layer depends on the type of problem you are trying to solve. For instance, in a binary classification problem, there would be a single output neuron, while in a multi-class classification problem with 10 classes, there would be 10 output neurons.

4. **Activation functions**: Activation functions are responsible for introducing non-linearity to the neural network. Non-linear activation functions allow the neural network to learn complex patterns in the data. Common activation functions used in Keras include ReLU, Sigmoid, and Tanh.

5. **Loss function**: The loss function is a measure of how well the neural network is performing. It calculates the difference between the actual output and the predicted output of the neural network. The goal of training the neural network is to minimize the loss function.

6. **Optimizer**: The optimizer is responsible for updating the weights of the neural network during the training process, to minimize the loss function. Common optimizers used in Keras include Stochastic Gradient Descent (SGD), Adam, and RMSprop.

Overall, the composition of a neural network in Keras depends on the problem you are trying to solve, the structure of the data, and the complexity of the model.

2.4   What are the different types of layers in Keras, and what are their purposes?

Keras is a high-level neural network API, and it provides a wide range of layers for building deep neural networks. Every layer is designed to handle a specific type of input, and applies a mathematical operation to transform the data into a more useful representation. Here are some of the most common types of layers in Keras and their purpose:

1. Dense Layer: The dense layer is also known as a fully connected layer. It's the most common type of layer that connects each neuron in one layer to all the neurons in the next layer. The dense layer can be used for classification, regression, and multi-class problems.

2. Convolutional Layer: The convolutional layer is the main building block of a Convolutional Neural Network (CNN). It applies a convolution operation to the input image, which helps detect local patterns and features. The convolutional layer works well for image and video recognition problems.

3. Recurrent Layer: The recurrent layer is used for sequential data learning, such as time-series data and natural language processing. It maintains an internal state that allows it to handle a sequence of input data.

4. Pooling Layer: The pooling layer is used to reduce the spatial size of an input feature map. It helps to make the model less sensitive to small variations in the input data and reduce the number of parameters in the model.

5. Dropout Layer: The dropout layer is a method for reducing overfitting during training. It randomly drops out some neurons during training to prevent them from overfitting on the training data. It helps to make the model more robust to variations in the input data.

6. Activation Layer: The activation layer applies a non-linear activation function to the output of the previous layer. Common activation functions include ReLU, Sigmoid, and Tanh. The activation layer introduces non-linearity into the model, allowing it to learn complex patterns and relationships.

In summary, Keras provides a variety of layers that can be used for building complex neural networks. Choosing the right layer for the specific problem is essential for achieving high accuracy and reducing overfitting.

2.5   How do you initialize a Sequential model in Keras, and what is its purpose?

A Sequential model in Keras is a linear stack of neural network layers, in which the output of one layer is passed as input to the next layer. The Sequential model is the simplest and most common way of building a deep learning model in Keras.

To initialize a Sequential model in Keras, you can use the 'Sequential()' function, which creates an empty Sequential model. Here is an example:

```
from tensorflow.keras.models import Sequential
model = Sequential()
```

Once you have created the Sequential model, you can add layers to it using the 'add()' method. For example, to add a Dense layer with 64 units and a ReLU activation function, you can do:

```
from tensorflow.keras.layers import Dense
model.add(Dense(64, activation='relu'))
```

You can add as many layers as you want to the Sequential model, and customize the number of units, activation functions, regularization techniques, and other hyperparameters to improve the model's performance on your specific task.

The purpose of initializing a Sequential model is to define the architecture and the parameters of the neural network, and to prepare it for training and prediction. By adding layers to the Sequential model, you are defining the sequence in which the data will be transformed by the network, and allowing it to learn the features and patterns in the data that are relevant to the task at hand. Once you have built the Sequential model, you can compile it with an optimizer, a loss function, and evaluation metrics, and then train it on the training data by calling the 'fit()' method. Finally, you can use the trained model to make predictions on new data by calling the 'predict()' method.

2.6 What is the role of activation functions in a neural network, and can you name a few common activation functions used in Keras?

The activation function plays a crucial role in neural networks by introducing non-linearity into the output of a neuron. The non-linear activation functions, such as sigmoid, tanh, ReLU, or LeakyReLU, are applied to the weighted sum of inputs and biases of a neuron to produce its output, which is then forwarded to the next layer of neurons in the network.

Without the activation function, the network would simply be performing linear transformations, and it would not be able to learn complex decision boundaries or patterns in the data. By applying an activation function, the output of a neuron can become a non-linear function of its inputs, which allows the network to learn complex and hierarchical representations of the data.

Here are the brief descriptions of a few common activation functions used in Keras:

1. Sigmoid: Sigmoid is a popular activation function used in binary output problems or where the output is a probability value. It squashes the input values within the range of 0 and 1, making it suitable for binary classification problems.

2. Tanh: Tanh is another popular activation function that squashes the input values between -1 and 1, making it suitable for regression problems.

3. ReLU (rectified linear unit): ReLU is currently one of the most widely used activation functions in deep learning, it is computationally efficient and doesn't suffer from vanishing gradient problems which occur with sigmoid and tanh functions. It sets all negative input values to zero and keeps the positive values unchanged.

4. LeakyReLU: LeakyReLU function is a variant of ReLU which introduces a small slope for negative input values rather than setting them to zero. It can help to avoid dead neurons that can sometimes

occur when using the ReLU activation function.

There are other activation functions also available which are used in specific scenarios. Choosing the right activation function is an important design decision to optimize the performance and accuracy of the neural network.

2.7   How do you compile a Keras model, and what are the key parameters required?

To compile a Keras model, you need to use the 'compile()' function that is part of the 'Model' class in Keras. The 'compile()' function allows you to specify the loss function, optimizer, and evaluation metrics that you want to use in your model.

Here is an example of how to compile a Keras model:

```
from keras.models import Sequential
from keras.layers import Dense

# Create a simple sequential model
model = Sequential()
model.add(Dense(64, input_dim=100, activation='relu'))
model.add(Dense(1, activation='sigmoid'))

# Compile the model
model.compile(loss='binary_crossentropy', optimizer='adam', metrics=['accuracy'
    ])
```

In the above example, we first create a simple sequential model with two dense layers. The 'input_dim' parameter specifies the number of input features to the model (in this case, 100), and we use the 'relu' activation function in the first layer and the 'sigmoid' activation function in the second layer.

To compile the model, we call the 'compile()' function on the 'model' object. We specify the 'binary_crossentropy' loss function, the 'adam' optimizer, and the 'accuracy' metric.

The 'loss' parameter specifies the objective function that we want to minimize during training. In this case, we are using binary cross-entropy, which is commonly used for binary classification problems.

The 'optimizer' parameter specifies the algorithm that we want to use to optimize the model parameters during training. Here, we are using the Adam optimizer, which is a popular choice for deep learning problems.

Finally, the 'metrics' parameter specifies the evaluation metrics that we want to use to monitor the performance of our model during training and testing. In this case, we are using the accuracy metric, which is a common metric for classification problems.

Overall, the key parameters required to compile a Keras model are the loss function, optimizer, and evaluation metrics. These parameters will depend on the specific problem you are working on and the architecture of your model.

2.8   What is the purpose of the fit() function in Keras, and what are some important parameters to consider when using it?

The fit() function in Keras is used to train a deep learning model on a given dataset. It takes care of the entire training process, including forward and backward propagation, optimization, and updating of the weights of the model.

The main purpose of the fit() function is to minimize the difference between the predicted and actual output of the model, and thus improve its accuracy. During the training process, the model is presented with examples from the training dataset, and it learns to predict the output for each example. Then, the weights of the model are updated, based on the difference between the predicted and actual output.

Some important parameters to consider when using the fit() function are:

- **X**: This parameter represents the input data that will be fed to the model during the training process. It should be an array or a matrix of shape (num_samples, input_shape).

- **y**: This parameter represents the target data that the model is trying to predict. It should be an array or a matrix of shape (num_samples, output_shape).

- **epochs**: This parameter specifies the number of times the entire dataset should be passed through the neural network during training. A higher number of epochs may lead to better accuracy, but also increases the risk of overfitting.

- **batch_size**: This parameter determines the number of samples that are passed through the network at once. A smaller batch size may lead to slower training, but can be helpful in avoiding overfitting.

- **validation_data**: This parameter allows you to specify a validation dataset, which is used to evaluate the performance of the model during training, and to detect overfitting.

- **callbacks**: This parameter represents a list of callbacks that are executed during training, and can be used to monitor the progress of the training process, save the weights of the model, etc.

In general, it is important to carefully select the values of these parameters in order to achieve the best possible performance from your model.

2.9 Can you explain the role of optimizers in Keras, and provide examples of some commonly used optimizers?

Optimizers in Keras are essential components in the process of training deep learning models. They determine the way in which the model learns the patterns in the input data and updates the weights of the neural network during backpropagation. The objective of any optimizer is to minimize the loss function for the given problem by modifying the weights of the model.

There are several commonly used optimizers in Keras, each with its own unique approach to updating the weights of the neural network. Here are some examples:

1. Stochastic Gradient Descent (SGD): This is the most basic optimizer used in deep learning. It updates the weights of the neural network based on the gradient of the loss function with respect to the weights. This optimizer works well for simple problems, but it can be slow to converge for more complex problems.

2. Adam: This is an adaptive optimizer that adjusts the learning rate according to the gradients of the previous time steps. It can converge faster than SGD and is widely used in many deep learning applications.

3. RMSprop: This optimizer also adjusts the learning rate, but it uses a moving average of the squared gradients to compute the update. It can converge faster than SGD and is particularly useful for problems with sparse gradients.

4. Adagrad: This optimizer adapts the learning rate for each parameter based on the historical gradients. It is particularly useful for problems with sparse gradients, but it can also suffer from a decreasing learning rate.

5. Adadelta: This optimizer is an extension of Adagrad that rectifies the problem of decreasing learning rates by using a moving window of the past gradients.

Overall, the choice of optimizer depends on the specific problem at hand, and it is often a matter of trial and error to find the best one for a particular application.

2.10 What is the difference between overfitting and underfitting in deep learning, and how can you prevent them in a Keras model?

Overfitting and underfitting are two issues that can occur in deep learning models, which can lead to poor performance.

Underfitting occurs when the model is too simple to capture the complexity of the data and it fails to learn the underlying patterns in the data. This results in poor performance on both the training and test data. In other words, the model doesn't generalize well to unseen data. This can often be seen in cases where the training data is not representative of the entire dataset, or when the model is not complex enough.

Overfitting, on the other hand, occurs when the model is too complex and starts to fit the noise in the training data rather than the underlying patterns. As a result, the model performs very well on the training data but performs poorly on the test data. In other words, the model doesn't generalize well to unseen data. Overfitting often occurs when the model has too many parameters or when the training dataset is too small to represent the entire dataset.

To prevent underfitting, it is often necessary to increase the complexity of the model. This can be done by adding additional layers or by increasing the number of nodes in the layers. Additionally, increasing the number of epochs or increasing the size of the training dataset can also help to prevent underfitting.

To prevent overfitting, there are several techniques that can be used. One popular method is to use regularization techniques, such as L1 or L2 regularization, which help to prevent the model from fitting the noise in the training data. Dropout is another technique that can be used to prevent overfitting by randomly dropping out units during training, which forces the model to learn more robust features. Another technique is early stopping, which stops training the model as soon as the validation loss starts to increase.

In Keras, regularization techniques can be added to the layers using the 'kernel_regularizer' and 'bias_regularizer' parameters. Dropout can be added using the 'Dropout' layer. Early stopping can be implemented using the 'EarlyStopping' callback. By applying these techniques, the model can be trained to generalize well to unseen data and prevent underfitting and overfitting.

2.11 What are loss functions, and why are they important in Keras? Can you provide examples of some commonly used loss functions?

In Keras, loss functions represent measures of how well a neural network is approximating the target function during training. The aim of training is to minimize this loss function as much as possible by adjusting the model parameters, such as weights and biases.

The loss function takes two inputs: - the predicted output of the neural network - the true output, which is the ground-truth label for that particular example

The loss function will then output a scalar value that indicates how well the network's output matches the true output, and this value acts as an indicator of the network's performance. The optimizer uses this value to update the weights and biases of the network to improve its performance.

Keras provides a wide range of loss functions that are tailored for different types of problems, such as classification, regression, and sequence prediction. Some commonly used loss functions are:

- Mean Squared Error (MSE): Used for regression problems, where the target output is continuous. This loss function computes the squared difference between the predicted output and the true output, averaged over all training examples, and gives importance to large differences.

- Mean Absolute Error (MAE): Also used for regression problems, this loss function computes the absolute difference between the predicted output and the true output, averaged over all training examples. It gives equal importance to small and large differences, and is less sensitive to outliers than MSE.

- Binary Cross Entropy (BCE): Used for binary classification problems, where the target output is either 0 or 1. This loss function measures the difference between the predicted probability of the positive class (class 1) and the true probability, and is commonly used with sigmoid activation in the last layer.

- Categorical Cross Entropy (CCE): Used for multi-class classification problems, where the target output is one-hot encoded. This loss function measures the difference between the predicted probability distribution over all classes and the true probability distribution, and is commonly used with softmax activation in the last layer.

These are just a few examples of the many loss functions available in Keras, and choosing the right one depends on the problem at hand.

2.12 What is the purpose of the evaluate() function in Keras, and what information does it provide?

The 'evaluate()' function in Keras is a method that is used to calculate the performance of a trained machine learning model on a given dataset. The main purpose of the 'evaluate()' function is to provide an estimate of the model's accuracy, and several other metrics of interest, such as precision, recall, and F1 score.

When evaluating a model using this function, the user can specify a test dataset, which is usually a subset of the data that was not used to train the model. The function then passes this dataset through the model and calculates metrics such as accuracy, loss, and others, based on how well the model is able to predict the output values of the test data.

The 'evaluate()' method returns an array containing the values of the metrics that were calculated (in the same order they were specified during the compilation of the model), allowing for the creation of graphs or summaries of the model's performance. Additionally, Keras will output the loss and any other metrics specified in the compilation step during training.

Here's an example:

```
# compile the model
model.compile(optimizer='adam', loss='binary_crossentropy', metrics=['accuracy'
    ])

# train the model
```

```
model.fit(X_train, y_train)

# evaluate the model on a test set
test_loss, test_acc = model.evaluate(X_test, y_test)
print('Test␣accuracy:', test_acc)
```

In the example above, 'X_train' and 'y_train' represent the training dataset and its corresponding labels, respectively; 'X_test' and 'y_test' are the test dataset and its labels, respectively. The 'compile()' function applies a gradient descent algorithm with the adaptive moment estimation optimizer, cross entropy loss function as well as an accuracy metric specified w.r.t binary class. While the 'fit()' function trains the model according to the dataset passed as input. The 'evaluate()' function is then called to calculate the model's performance on the test set, and the resulting test accuracy is printed to the console.

2.13   How do you use the predict() function in Keras, and what does it return?

The 'predict()' function in Keras is used to obtain predictions from a trained neural network model. Specifically, given a set of inputs, it will produce a set of output predictions.

Here is an example of how to use 'predict()':

```
# Load the model from disk
model = load_model('my_model.h5')

# Generate some input data (e.g. test data)
X_test = generate_test_data()

# Use the predict function to obtain output predictions for the input data
y_pred = model.predict(X_test)
```

Here, we first load the trained model from disk using the 'load_model()' function in Keras. We then generate some test data as input for the model using a hypothetical function 'generate_test_data()'. Finally, we use the 'predict()' function to obtain output predictions for our test data, which are stored in 'y_pred'.

The 'predict()' function returns a numpy array of predicted outputs for the given input data. The array will have a shape that depends on the number of input samples and the number of output units in the model. For example, if our model had a single output unit, the output array would be a one-dimensional numpy array with a length equal to the number of input samples. If our model had multiple output units, the output array would be a two-dimensional numpy array with dimensions of [number of input samples, number of output units].

2.14 What is the role of batch size in training a Keras model, and how does it affect model performance?

Batch size is an important hyperparameter in training a Keras model. It determines the number of samples that will be propagated through the neural network before performing a single update of the model parameters (weights and biases). In other words, it defines how many samples are processed at once in each epoch.

The batch size can significantly impact the training process and model performance. Here are some of the key effects of the batch size:

1. **Memory usage:** Larger batch sizes require more memory resources to store the intermediate activations, gradients, and weight updates during training. If the batch size exceeds the memory capacity of your system, you may need to reduce the batch size or use a generator that loads the data on-the-fly during training.

2. **Training speed:** Larger batch sizes can increase the training speed by reducing the number of weight updates per epoch. However, if the batch size is too large, it may slow down the convergence of the model as the updates become less frequent. In contrast, smaller batch sizes may take longer to train but can provide better convergence, especially when dealing with complex or noisy data.

3. **Generalization performance:** The choice of batch size can impact the generalization performance of the model. Small batch sizes can provide more stochasticity and increase the diversity of the training samples considered during each epoch. This can help prevent overfitting and improve the model's ability to generalize to new data. In contrast, large batch sizes can result in a smoother gradient de-

scent path, which can lead to overfitting and reduced generalization performance.

4. **Batch normalization:** Batch size can also impact batch normalization, a popular technique to accelerate the convergence of deep neural networks. Batch normalization calculates the mean and variance of the activations across a batch of samples and uses them to normalize the activations. Larger batch sizes can provide more reliable estimates of the mean and variance, which results in more stable and accurate normalization.

To summarize, choosing the right batch size depends on the specific characteristics of the dataset, architecture, and available hardware. It's a good practice to experiment with different batch sizes and monitor the training process, performance metrics, and convergence behavior to find the optimal value.

2.15   How do you save and load a trained Keras model?

To save a trained Keras model, you can use the 'model.save()' method, which stores the model architecture, weights, and optimizer state in a single file format called HDF5.

Here's an example:

```
from tensorflow import keras

# Create and train a Keras model
model = keras.models.Sequential([
    keras.layers.Dense(10, input_shape=(20,), activation="relu"),
    keras.layers.Dense(1, activation="sigmoid")
])
model.compile(loss="binary_crossentropy", optimizer="sgd")
model.fit(x_train, y_train, epochs=10)

# Save the trained model
model.save("my_model.h5")
```

To load a saved model, you can use the 'keras.models.load_model()' method, which loads the architecture, weights, and optimizer state from the HDF5 file.

Here's an example:

```
# Load a saved Keras model
model = keras.models.load_model("my_model.h5")

# Make predictions with the loaded model
y_pred = model.predict(x_test)
```

Note that when you load a model, you should use the same version of Keras and TensorFlow that were used to save the model, otherwise loading the model may fail.

2.16 What is the purpose of using callbacks in Keras, and can you provide examples of some commonly used callbacks?

Callbacks are functions that are called during the training process in Keras, which can be used to keep track of important metrics, apply regularization, or alter the learning rate. These functions are called at certain stages of the training process and can be used to monitor and even modify the behaviour of the training algorithm.

Commonly used callbacks include:

1. ModelCheckpoint: This callback saves the model after every epoch, which is useful in case the training process is interrupted or there is a power failure during the training process. It saves the best weights of the model, and the saved model can be loaded and used for further training, for deploying or for prediction.

2. EarlyStopping: This callback monitors a specified metric and stops the training process when the monitored metric doesn't improve for a specific number of epochs. This is useful when you want to avoid overfitting the data and stop training early when the model is not improving its validation performance.

3. ReduceLROnPlateau: This callback reduces the learning rate when the validation metric doesn't improve for a specified number of epochs. This is useful for fine-tuning the model, as it allows for smaller and smaller steps to be taken towards the optimal model weights, which can help avoid over-shooting the minimum.

4. TensorBoard: This callback logs the training process and can be used to visualize the metrics in TensorBoard, an interactive visualization tool offered by TensorFlow. This allows you to monitor the progress of your model during training and helps you to identify the weaknesses in your model.

5. CSVLogger: This callback logs the loss and evaluation metrics into a CSV file, which can be easily visualized using Excel, LibreOffice Calc or other spreadsheet software.

Overall, callbacks are very useful in Keras, allowing you to monitor the training process, configure early stopping, track metrics and optimize hyperparameters automatically.

2.17   What are the differences between the Keras functional API and the Sequential model?

Keras provides two different ways to define the architecture of a neural network: the Sequential Model and the Functional API. Both of these methods can be used to create a Keras model, but they have some differences:

1. Sequential Model: The Sequential Model is a linear stack of layers, and it's the simplest and most common way to build a neural network in Keras. You can add layers to the model one by one, and each layer will be connected to the previous layer automatically. It's easy to use and understand, especially for beginners. Additionally, the Sequential model supports most of the common layers that are used in deep learning. However, it's not suitable for building complex models since it's not flexible enough.

Here's an example of how to create a Sequential model in Keras:

```
from keras.models import Sequential
from keras.layers import Dense

model = Sequential()

model.add(Dense(units=64, activation='relu', input_dim=100))
model.add(Dense(units=10, activation='softmax'))
```

2. Functional API: The Functional API allows you to define complex models that have multiple inputs, outputs, and layers that are not connected sequentially. It's more flexible than the Sequential model, and it can handle more complex architectures such as multi-input and multi-output models. Moreover, the Functional API enables you to define shared layers or weight-sharing models, which can be useful in some situations. However, it can be more challenging to use and understand, especially for beginners.

Here's an example of how to create a simple model using the Functional API in Keras:

```
from keras.layers import Input, Dense
from keras.models import Model

inputs = Input(shape=(100,))
x = Dense(units=64, activation='relu')(inputs)
predictions = Dense(units=10, activation='softmax')(x)
model = Model(inputs=inputs, outputs=predictions)
```

In summary, the Sequential model is a basic and easy-to-use way of building a neural network in Keras, while the Functional API is a more flexible way of building complex models with multiple inputs and outputs. If your model has a straightforward architecture, the Sequential model is generally easier to use. However, if you need a more complex architecture with multiple inputs, outputs, or shared layers, the Functional API is the way to go.

2.18 How do you apply regularization techniques in Keras, such as L1 and L2 regularization?

Regularization is a technique used in deep learning to prevent overfitting and improve the generalization performance of a model. Keras provides several regularization mechanisms that can be easily applied to your neural network layers.

The most commonly used regularization techniques in Keras are L1 and L2 regularization. Let's look at how to apply them in Keras.

1. L1 regularization: L1 regularization adds a penalty for the absolute value of the model weights. The L1 regularization function is added to

the loss function of the neural network, and the optimizer minimizes the total loss. In Keras, you can apply L1 regularization by setting the 'kernel_regularizer' parameter in a Dense or Conv2D layer.

Example:

```
from keras import regularizers
from keras.layers import Dense

model = Sequential()
model.add(Dense(64, input_dim=784, activation='relu', kernel_regularizer=
    regularizers.l1(0.01)))
model.add(Dense(64, activation='relu', kernel_regularizer=regularizers.l1(0.01))
    )
model.add(Dense(10, activation='softmax'))
```

Here, we have applied L1 regularization to both the Dense layers by setting the 'kernel_regularizer' parameter. The value 0.01 represents the amount of regularization to apply.

2. L2 regularization: L2 regularization adds a penalty for the square of the model weights. Just like L1 regularization, L2 regularization function is added to the loss function of the neural network, and the optimizer minimizes the total loss. In Keras, you can apply L2 regularization by setting the 'kernel_regularizer' parameter in a Dense or Conv2D layer, similar to L1 regularization.

Example:

```
from keras import regularizers
from keras.layers import Dense

model = Sequential()
model.add(Dense(64, input_dim=784, activation='relu', kernel_regularizer=
    regularizers.l2(0.01)))
model.add(Dense(64, activation='relu', kernel_regularizer=regularizers.l2(0.01))
    )
model.add(Dense(10, activation='softmax'))
```

Here, we have applied L2 regularization to both the Dense layers by setting the 'kernel_regularizer' parameter. The value 0.01 represents the amount of regularization to apply.

In summary, regularization is an important technique to combat over-fitting in deep learning. In Keras, you can easily apply L1 and L2 regularization to your neural network layers by setting the 'kernel_regularizer' parameter in a Dense or Conv2D layer.

2.19   Can you explain the concept of early stopping in Keras, and how it helps prevent overfitting?

Early stopping is a regularization technique used in Keras that helps to prevent overfitting of a model. It involves monitoring the performance of the model on a validation set during training, and stopping the training process once the model's performance on the validation set starts to decrease or stops improving.

The idea behind early stopping is that, as the training progresses, the model usually starts to overfit to the training data, which results in a decrease in its generalization performance. This happens when the model learns to memorize the training data instead of learning its underlying patterns.

Early stopping works by monitoring the validation loss (or any other validation metric) during training, and stopping the training process once this loss starts to increase consistently. This is done by comparing the current validation loss with the best validation loss achieved so far. If the current validation loss is higher than the best validation loss, the training process is stopped and the best model parameters are saved.

The main advantage of early stopping is that it helps to prevent overfitting by stopping the training process at the optimal point, before the model starts to memorize the training data.

Here is an example of how to implement early stopping in Keras:

```
from keras.callbacks import EarlyStopping

# Define the EarlyStopping callback
early_stop = EarlyStopping(monitor='val_loss', patience=5)

# Train the model with early stopping
model.fit(X_train, y_train, epochs=1000, validation_split=0.2, callbacks=[
    early_stop])
```

In the example above, we define an EarlyStopping callback that will monitor the validation loss and stop the training process if the validation loss does not improve for five consecutive epochs. Then, we include the early_stop callback in the fit method as a list of callbacks. This way, Keras will monitor the validation loss during training and stop the process when the EarlyStopping condition is met.

Overall, early stopping is an important technique for preventing over-fitting of deep learning models, and Keras makes its implementation a straightforward process.

2.20 What is transfer learning, and how can you implement it using Keras?

Transfer Learning is a deep learning technique where you use pre-trained models as the starting point for your own training tasks. The pre-trained models are trained on large datasets and are very good at capturing high-level features from images. Instead of starting the training of a new deep learning model from scratch, you can leverage the pre-trained models and adjust the weights to fit the new task. This saves you lots of time and effort, and also increases the accuracy of the model since the pre-trained model has already learned a lot of features and patterns.

In Keras, transfer learning is very easy to implement. There are two main ways to use transfer learning in Keras: fine-tuning and feature extraction.

In fine-tuning transfer learning, you start with a pre-trained model and then fine-tune it on a new dataset. Fine-tuning consists of re-placing the last layer of the pre-trained model with a new layer that is adapted to the new dataset. You can then train the entire model on the new dataset, or freeze some of the layers in the pre-trained model and train only the new layer. This will allow the model to learn new features specific to the new dataset while retaining the important features learned on the pre-trained model.

Here's an example of fine-tuning using Keras:

```
# Load the pre-trained model
from keras.applications import VGG16
vgg_model = VGG16(weights='imagenet', include_top=False, input_shape=(224, 224,
    3))

# Freeze some layers in the pre-trained model
for layer in vgg_model.layers[:15]:
    layer.trainable = False

# Add a new layer to the model
```

```
from keras.models import Sequential
from keras.layers import Dense, Flatten
model = Sequential()
model.add(vgg_model)
model.add(Flatten())
model.add(Dense(256, activation='relu'))
model.add(Dense(1, activation='sigmoid'))

# Compile the model
model.compile(optimizer='adam', loss='binary_crossentropy', metrics=['accuracy'
    ])

# Train the model on the new dataset
model.fit(x_train, y_train, epochs=10, batch_size=32, validation_data=(x_val,
    y_val))
```

In feature extraction transfer learning, you use the pre-trained model as a feature extractor, and extract the features from the pre-trained model to train a new model on a new dataset. The pre-trained model is used to extract features from the input images, and then a new classifier is trained based on these features. In Keras, this involves freezing all the layers in the pre-trained model and then adding a new classifier on top of it. The pre-trained model is then used to extract features from the images, and the classifier is trained on these features.

Here's an example of feature extraction using Keras:

```
# Load the pre-trained model
from keras.applications import VGG16
model = VGG16(weights='imagenet', include_top=False, input_shape=(224, 224, 3))
for layer in model.layers:
    layer.trainable = False

# Extract features from the pre-trained model
train_features = model.predict(x_train)
val_features = model.predict(x_val)

# Train a new classifier on the extracted features
new_model = Sequential()
new_model.add(Flatten(input_shape=train_features.shape[1:]))
new_model.add(Dense(256, activation='relu'))
new_model.add(Dense(1, activation='sigmoid'))
new_model.compile(optimizer='adam', loss='binary_crossentropy', metrics=['
    accuracy'])

# Train the model on the extracted features
new_model.fit(train_features, y_train, epochs=10, batch_size=32, validation_data
    =(val_features, y_val))
```

Overall, transfer learning is a powerful technique for building deep learning models that can help improve model performance and reduce training time. In Keras, there are several pre-trained models such as VGG, ResNet, MobileNet, etc., which you can use for transfer learning.

Chapter 3

Intermediate

3.1 What is the difference between a Dense layer and a Convolutional layer in Keras, and when would you use each?

Dense layers and Convolutional layers are two commonly used layer types in deep learning models built using Keras.

A Dense layer is also known as a fully connected layer. In a Dense layer, each neuron is connected to all the neurons in the previous layer. The output of the dense layer is determined by the weights associated with each of these connections and the bias of each neuron in the layer. Dense layers are commonly used in the output layer of many models, and also in the hidden layers of models designed to process tabular data, like a spreadsheet. An example use-case of a Dense layer is image classification on tabular data, such as the Fashion-MNIST dataset.

In contrast, a Convolutional layer is designed to process image data. Convolutional layers are built around the concept of learning features from an image, and they apply a set of filters to the input image. Each filter generates a feature map highlighting the presence of a particular feature. Convolutional layers have a relatively small number of weights compared to a dense layer, and they perform the necessary convolution operation that helps some important features to be captured. Convolutional layers are organized in a hierarchical fashion, usually followed by dense layers, which learn from the output of the feature maps produced by convolution layers. Convolutional layers are commonly used in convolutional neural networks (CNNs), which often achieve state-of-the-art performance on image classification tasks.

The main difference between Dense and Convolutional layers lies in how they process the input data. While Dense layers process all dimensions of the input data, Convolutional layers take advantage of local correlations in the input. In other words, Convolutional layers look for meaningful patterns in subsections of the input image, while Dense layers consider the entire input at once. This makes Convolutional layers well-suited for image data where local patterns capture important information about the object or scene.

In conclusion, Dense layers and Convolutional layers are used for different purposes in Keras models. Dense layers are used to process tabular data, while Convolutional layers are designed for image data. Both layers can be used in combination to form powerful neural networks for both classification and regression tasks.

3.2   Can you explain the concept of recurrent neural networks (RNNs) and how they can be implemented in Keras?

Recurrent neural networks (RNNs) are a type of neural network that can handle sequential data, such as time series data or natural language text. They differ from traditional feedforward neural networks in that they have loops in them, which allow them to pass information from earlier time steps to later time steps.

The basic building block of an RNN is the "cell," which contains a hidden state that is updated at each time step. The updated hidden state is then used to make a prediction for the current time step.

One common type of RNN cell is the Long Short-Term Memory

(LSTM) cell, which allows information to be selectively remembered or forgotten over time. Another type is the Gated Recurrent Unit (GRU) cell, which is similar to LSTM but has fewer parameters.

In Keras, you can implement an RNN by using one of the built-in RNN layers, such as 'LSTM' or 'GRU'. For example, here is some code to define an LSTM-based RNN to classify movie reviews:

```
from keras.layers import LSTM, Embedding, Dense
from keras.models import Sequential

model = Sequential()
model.add(Embedding(max_features, 128))
model.add(LSTM(128, dropout=0.2, recurrent_dropout=0.2))
model.add(Dense(1, activation='sigmoid'))
```

Here, we first add an 'Embedding' layer to convert our input data (movie reviews) into dense vector embeddings. Then, we add an 'LSTM' layer with 128 hidden units and a dropout rate of 0.2 to prevent overfitting. Finally, we add a 'Dense' layer with a sigmoid activation function to output a probability for each review.

Overall, RNNs are a powerful tool for handling sequential data, and Keras provides an easy way to implement them in practice.

3.3   What is the purpose of dropout layers in Keras, and how do they help prevent overfitting?

Dropout is a regularization technique used in deep learning models to prevent overfitting. In Keras, dropout layers can be added to a model to help improve the generalization capabilities of the model.

The main idea behind dropout is to randomly drop (i.e., set to zero) a certain percentage of the neurons in a layer during each training iteration. This "dropping out" of neurons forces the network to learn a more robust representation of the input data. Since the neurons are randomly dropped out, the remaining neurons need to compensate for the missing ones, leading to a reduction in over-reliance on particular neurons. This helps prevent the model from fitting too closely to the training data and failing to generalize to new input data.

By reducing the complexity of the model, dropout helps to prevent overfitting and improves the model's ability to generalize to new data. Dropout is particularly effective when the model is overparametrized, and adding more data is not feasible.

In Keras, dropout layers can be added to a model using the 'Dropout' layer. For example, to add a dropout layer to a model, you can use the following code:

```
from keras.models import Sequential
from keras.layers import Dense, Dropout

model = Sequential()
model.add(Dense(64, activation='relu', input_shape=(input_shape,)))
model.add(Dropout(0.5))
model.add(Dense(32, activation='relu'))
model.add(Dense(output_dim, activation='softmax'))
```

In this example, a dropout layer with a dropout rate of 0.5 is added after the first dense layer. The dropout layer randomly sets 50% of the activations to zero during each training iteration, helping to prevent overfitting.

3.4   How do you handle imbalanced datasets in Keras, and what techniques can you use to address this issue?

Handling imbalanced datasets is a common problem in Machine Learning, and Keras provides several techniques to address this issue. Imbalanced datasets occur when the number of observations in the minority class is significantly lower than the number of observations in the majority class.

Here are some techniques that you can use to handle imbalanced datasets in Keras:

1. Resampling: You can either undersample the majority class or oversample the minority class. Undersampling involves randomly removing observations from the majority class, whereas oversampling involves replicating minority class observations until they are in the same proportion as the majority class. This technique can be performed using Keras 'fit_generator' function's 'steps_per_epoch' ar-

gument and 'ImageDataGenerator' from 'keras.preprocessing.image' function.

2. Class Weights: In Keras, the 'class_weights' argument lets you assign a weight to each class to balance out the imbalanced dataset. This approach gives more importance to the minority class during model training, and can be done with the help of the 'fit' method in Keras.

3. Synthetic data generation: Another approach is to create synthetic data for the minority class by applying data augmentation techniques such as rotation, zooming, cropping, and flipping. Keras provides an 'ImageDataGenerator' class that can be used for data augmentation.

4. Ensemble Methods: Ensemble approaches like Bagging or Boosting techniques can also be used to handle imbalanced datasets in Keras. These methods combine models or predictions from multiple models that were trained on different subsets of the data, in order to increase accuracy and reduce bias.

Example of implementing these techniques in Keras:

```
# import necessary libraries
import keras
from keras.utils import to_categorical
from imblearn.over_sampling import RandomOverSampler

# load the dataset
(X_train, y_train), (X_test, y_test) = keras.datasets.fashion_mnist.load_data()

# oversample the minority class
ros = RandomOverSampler()
X_train_resampled, y_train_resampled = ros.fit_resample(X_train.reshape(-1, 784)
    , y_train)
X_train_resampled = X_train_resampled.reshape(-1, 28, 28, 1)

# convert class vectors to binary class matrices
num_classes = 10
y_train_binary = to_categorical(y_train_resampled, num_classes)
y_test_binary = to_categorical(y_test, num_classes)

# create data generator object for image augmentation
datagen = keras.preprocessing.image.ImageDataGenerator(rotation_range=20,
    zoom_range=0.2,
                                                       width_shift_range=0.1,
    height_shift_range=0.1,
                                                       shear_range=0.15,
    horizontal_flip=True,
                                                       vertical_flip=True,
    fill_mode="nearest")

# create Keras model and compile it
model = keras.Sequential([...] )
model.compile(loss='categorical_crossentropy', optimizer='adam', metrics=['
    accuracy'])

# fit the model using class weights
```

```
class_weights = {0: 1.0, 1: 3.0, 2:4.0, 3:4.0, 4:4.0, 5:1.0, 6:2.0, 7:4.0,
    8:4.0, 9:1.0}
history = model.fit(datagen.flow(X_train_resampled, y_train_binary, batch_size
    =64),
                    epochs=50, validation_data=(X_test, y_test_binary),
    class_weight=class_weights)
```

In the above example, we applied oversampling using 'RandomOver-
Sampler()' to balance the classes, and created a 'ImageDataGenerator' object for data augmentation. We further used class weights
dictionary to apply more weight to minority classes during model
training.

Moreover, each specific dataset may require a different approach to
balance classes, and the above techniques just provide a starting point
to deal with imbalanced datasets in Keras.

3.5   What are the advantages of using batch normalization in Keras, and how do you implement it in a model?

Batch normalization is a popular technique used to improve the optimization and generalization properties of deep neural networks. It is
a process of adding an extra normalization step during training where
the mean and variance of each batch of inputs are computed and used
to standardize them.

The advantages of using batch normalization in Keras are as follows:

1. Faster convergence: Adding batch normalization to a neural network helps it converge faster. This is because it reduces the internal
covariate shift which refers to the changes in the distribution of the
activations of each layer that occur during training. By normalizing
the activations, the parameters of the layers in a network are updated
more consistently and quickly during training.

2. Improved generalization: Batch normalization regularizes the network by reducing overfitting. It does this by reducing the sensitivity
of the network's activations to the small changes in the input distribution. Hence, the network becomes more robust and generalizes

better to unseen data.

3. Better performance: Batch normalization can also lead to better performance. It allows the use of higher learning rates, which helps in the optimization process. Furthermore, it reduces the influence of the initialization of the network, making it less susceptible to parameter initialization issues.

To implement batch normalization in a Keras model, you can use the BatchNormalization layer. This is a layer that normalizes its inputs using statistics computed over a mini-batch of data. It can be added to any layer in the network as follows:

```
from keras.layers import BatchNormalization
from keras.models import Sequential
from keras.layers import Dense

# Define the model
model = Sequential()
model.add(Dense(64, input_shape=(100,)))
model.add(BatchNormalization())
model.add(Dense(64, activation='relu'))
model.add(BatchNormalization())
model.add(Dense(10, activation='softmax'))

# Compile the model
model.compile(optimizer='adam', loss='categorical_crossentropy', metrics=['
    accuracy'])
```

In the above example, batch normalization is added after each fully connected layer in the network. Additionally, the BatchNormalization layer has several parameters that can be configured to control its behavior, such as the momentum, epsilon, and beta_initializer. By tweaking these parameters, you can further optimize the performance of the network.

3.6   Can you explain the concept of gradient clipping in Keras, and why it might be useful during training?

Gradient clipping is a technique used during the training of deep neural networks that can help prevent the exploding gradient problem from occurring. During training, gradient descent is used to update the weights of the neural network by computing the gradients of the loss function with respect to the weights in each layer of the network.

However, in some cases, particularly with deep neural networks or networks with recurrent connections, these gradients can become very large, leading to numerical instability and slow convergence.

Gradient clipping is a simple yet powerful solution to this problem. The idea is to set a maximum threshold for the gradient magnitude, and if the gradient exceeds this threshold, the magnitude is truncated to the maximum value. This means that the step taken during gradient descent is limited, preventing it from becoming too large and destabilizing the optimization process.

In Keras, gradient clipping can be implemented by setting the 'clipnorm' or 'clipvalue' parameters in the optimizer class.

For example, to use gradient clipping with a maximum norm of 1.0, you can add the following line to your code:

```
from keras.optimizers import SGD
optimizer = SGD(lr=0.001, clipnorm=1.0)
```

The 'clipnorm' parameter sets the maximum L2 norm of the gradient vector. Alternatively, you can use the 'clipvalue' parameter to set the maximum absolute value of each individual gradient value.

There are several reasons why gradient clipping can be useful during training. Firstly, it can improve the stability and performance of the network by preventing numerical overflow or underflow. Secondly, it can allow the use of larger learning rates or longer training epochs, which may lead to better convergence and higher accuracy. Lastly, it can help to prevent the occurrence of exploding gradients, which can cause the training process to fail entirely.

3.7   How do you handle missing or corrupted data when preparing a dataset for a Keras model?

Handling missing or corrupted data is an important step in preparing a dataset for a Keras model. Here are some common approaches to address missing or corrupted data:

1. Removing missing or corrupted data: One way to handle missing or corrupted data is to simply remove it from the dataset. This approach is appropriate when the amount of missing or corrupted data is small and does not significantly impact the dataset's overall size. However, if the amount of missing or corrupted data is large, this approach can result in a significant loss of information.

2. Data imputation: Another approach to handling missing or corrupted data is to impute the missing or corrupted values with estimated values. Data imputation can take different forms depending on the nature of the data. For example, for quantitative data, a common imputation technique is mean imputation, where the missing values are replaced by the mean value of the available data. Alternatively, a regression model can be used to predict the missing values based on the other available data. For categorical data, common imputation techniques include mode imputation and k-nearest neighbor imputation.

3. Feature engineering: In some cases, missing or corrupted data can be used to create new features for the Keras model. For example, a missing value in a certain column can be replaced by a binary flag indicating whether the value was missing or not. Alternatively, a corrupted value can be replaced with a feature indicating how different it is from the other values in the same column.

4. Augmentation: Data augmentation techniques can be used to generate new sample data points, thereby minimizing the impact of missing or corrupted data on the model. For instance, in image processing tasks, data augmentation can be performed by rotating, flipping, zooming, or shifting the images to generate more varied samples.

In summary, handling missing or corrupted data is an essential step in preparing a dataset for a Keras model. The approach to take depends on the nature and amount of the missing or corrupted data, and several techniques exist, including data removal, data imputation, feature engineering, and data augmentation. It is important to choose the approach that best suits the problem at hand while ensuring the integrity of the dataset.

3.8   What is the purpose of an embedding layer in Keras, and when would you use one?

In Keras, an embedding layer is a layer that is used to convert high-dimensional discrete data, such as text or categorical data, into a lower-dimensional continuous vector representation, called an embedding. The purpose of an embedding layer is to map each discrete data point to a continuous vector space, where similar data points are located close to each other, and dissimilar data points are located far apart from each other.

The main benefit of using an embedding layer is that it allows the model to learn meaningful representations of the input features that can capture complex relationships between them. This can enable the model to make better predictions and generalize well to new, unseen data.

Here are some common use cases for using an embedding layer in Keras:

1. Text classification: In natural language processing tasks such as text classification, an embedding layer can be used to convert each word in the input text into a fixed-length vector. This allows the model to learn the underlying structure of the text by encoding information about each word's meaning and context.

2. Recommender systems: In recommender systems, an embedding layer can be used to encode user and item data, such as user IDs and item IDs, into a continuous vector space. This can enable the model to learn user and item representations that capture complex relationships between them, and can be used to make personalized recommendations.

3. Image classification: In image classification, an embedding layer can be used to take the output from a convolutional neural network (CNN) and convert it into a fixed-length vector representation. This can enable the model to learn representations of the image that can capture high-level features, such as edges and shapes, as well as more abstract concepts such as textures and patterns.

In summary, an embedding layer in Keras is a powerful tool for learning meaningful representations of high-dimensional, discrete data. It can be used in a variety of applications, including text classification, recommender systems, and image classification, to improve model performance and generalization.

3.9   How do you perform hyperparameter tuning in Keras to optimize the performance of a model?

Hyperparameter tuning is a crucial component of building a deep learning model. Deep learning models contain a large number of hyperparameters that can dramatically impact their performance. There are several ways to perform hyperparameter tuning in Keras to achieve optimal performance, and here are some common ones:

1. Grid Search: One of the most popular methods of hyperparameter tuning is by using a grid search approach. In this method, you set up a grid with different hyperparameter combinations, and then test the performance of the model with each combination. You can use scikit-learn's 'GridSearchCV' function to do this.

For example, let's say you're training a convolution neural network (CNN) for image classification, and you want to find the optimal values for the learning rate, batch size and number of epochs. You can create a grid search object like this:

```
from keras.wrappers.scikit_learn import KerasClassifier
from sklearn.model_selection import GridSearchCV
from keras.models import Sequential
from keras.layers import Dense, Conv2D, Flatten

def create_model(lr=0.001, batch_size=32):
    model = Sequential()
    model.add(Conv2D(32, kernel_size=(3,3), activation='relu', input_shape=(28,
      28, 1)))
    model.add(Flatten())
    model.add(Dense(10, activation='softmax'))
    model.compile(optimizer=Adam(lr=lr), loss='categorical_crossentropy',
      metrics=['accuracy'])
    return model

# define the grid search parameters
param_grid = {'lr': [0.001, 0.01, 0.1],
              'batch_size': [16, 32, 64],
              'epochs': [10, 20, 30]}
```

```
# create the model
model = KerasClassifier(build_fn=create_model, verbose=0)

grid = GridSearchCV(estimator=model, param_grid=param_grid, n_jobs=-1, cv=3)
grid_result = grid.fit(X_train, y_train)

print("Best:␣%f␣using␣%s" % (grid_result.best_score_, grid_result.best_params_))
```

This code creates a CNN model, and a grid search object with different values for learning rate, batch size and number epochs as defined in 'param_grid' dictionary. We use KerasClassifier to wrap the model so we can use the 'GridSearchCV' function from scikit-learn. Finally, the grid search is executed on the dataset with 'X_train' and 'y_train' and returns the best hyperparameters combination and its corresponding performance.

2. Random Search: Another approach is to perform a random search, which searches the hyperparameters space randomly instead of exhaustively. This method can potentially result in better performance than grid search because it allows for a more extensive search of the hyperparameters space and is often more computationally efficient. You can use scikit-learn's 'RandomizedSearchCV' function to perform a random search.

```
from sklearn.model_selection import RandomizedSearchCV

# define the grid search parameters
param_grid = {'lr': [0.001, 0.01, 0.1],
              'batch_size': [16, 32, 64],
              'epochs': [10, 20, 30]}

# create the model
model = KerasClassifier(build_fn=create_model, verbose=0)

random_search = RandomizedSearchCV(estimator=model, param_distributions=
     param_grid, n_iter=100, cv=3, verbose=2, random_state=42, n_jobs=-1)
random_search.fit(X_train, y_train)

print("Best:␣%f␣using␣%s" % (random_search.best_score_, random_search.
     best_params_))
```

This code is similar to the previous example, but the 'GridSearchCV' function has been replaced with 'RandomizedSearchCV' function. You can also notice that 'n_iter' is added, which denotes the number of random combinations to try.

3. Bayesian optimization: This approach is more advanced and typically takes longer to compute while yielding better results than Grid or Random search. It involves creating a probability model that can predict the performance of the model with different hyperparameters configurations without actually running it. The probability model is

then used to sequentially suggest new combinations of hyperparameters based on the expected improvement, resulting in better results. There are several libraries in Python that can help implement such optimization like hyperopt, Optuna, Keras Tuner, or scikit-optimize, but Keras Tuner provides an easy-to-use interface for tuning Keras models.

Here's an example of how to use Keras Tuner, which takes care of using different Bayesian optimization methods, to tune a model.

```
!pip install keras-tuner

import keras_tuner as kt

def model_builder(hp):

    model = Sequential()
    model.add(Conv2D(32, kernel_size=(3,3), activation='relu', input_shape=(28,
      28, 1)))
    model.add(Flatten())
    model.add(Dense(10, activation='softmax'))

    # Tune the number of units of the first Dense layer
    # Choose from 32, 64, 128, or 256
    hp_units = hp.Choice('units', values=[32, 64, 128, 256])
    model.add(Dense(units=hp_units, activation='relu'))

    # Tune the learning rate for the optimizer
    # Choose from 0.0001, 0.001, 0.01, or 0.1
    hp_learning_rate = hp.Choice('learning_rate', values=[1e-4, 1e-3, 1e-2, 1e
      -1])
    model.compile(optimizer=Adam(lr=hp_learning_rate), loss='
      categorical_crossentropy', metrics=['accuracy'])

    return model

tuner = kt.Hyperband(model_builder,
                     objective='val_accuracy',
                     max_epochs=10,
                     factor=3,
                     directory='my_dir',
                     project_name='my_project')

tuner.search(X_train, y_train, epochs=10, validation_data=(X_test, y_test))

best_hps = tuner.get_best_hyperparameters(num_trials = 1)[0]
print(f"The optimal number of units is {best_hps.get('units')} and the optimal 
    learning rate for the optimizer is {best_hps.get('learning_rate')}")
```

This code builds a classifier model, but it tunes the number of units of the first dense layer and the learning rate of the optimizer instead of more common hyperparameters. The 'model_builder' function defines a model with tunable hyperparameters. Keras Tuner's 'Hyperband' class is used to perform hyperparameter search. It uses asymmetric training and early stopping to search asynchronously through the space of models.

In summary, hyperparameter tuning is an iterative process that requires experimentation and patience. By using the mentioned methods, you can find the best possible hyperparameters combination to improve the performance of your model.

3.10   Can you explain the concept of a 1D, 2D, and 3D convolution in Keras, and provide an example of when each might be used?

Convolutional Neural Networks (CNNs) are widely used for image and signal processing tasks, where they are able to learn and extract features. Convolutional layers in Keras can perform 1D, 2D, or 3D convolutions, depending on the type of input data.

1D convolution: This is used for processing sequential data. The input data is typically a time series, audio signal, or one-dimensional signal data. The kernel slides along the input data in one dimension, performing the dot product between the kernel and input at each step. A common application of 1D convolution is in natural language processing, where a sequence of words in a sentence can be convolved to extract important features.

Example:

```
from keras.layers import Conv1D

model = Sequential()
model.add(Conv1D(filters=64, kernel_size=3, activation='relu', input_shape
    =(100,1)))
```

In the above example, we define a 1D convolution layer with 64 filters and kernel size of 3. The input shape is (100,1), indicating a sequence of 100 time steps and 1 input channel.

2D convolution: This is used for processing image data. The input data is typically a 2D matrix (e.g. an image) with one or more channels. The kernel slides in two dimensions over the image, performing the dot product between the kernel and input at each step. 2D convolution is commonly used in tasks such as object detection or image classification.

Example:

```
from keras.layers import Conv2D

model = Sequential()
model.add(Conv2D(filters=32, kernel_size=(3, 3), activation='relu', input_shape
    =(28, 28, 1)))
```

In the above example, we define a 2D convolution layer with 32 filters and kernel size of (3, 3). The input shape is (28, 28, 1), indicating an image with dimensions of 28x28 and 1 input channel.

3D convolution: This is used for processing volumetric data. The input data is typically a 3D matrix (e.g. medical imaging data such as CT scans), with one or more channels. The kernel slides in three dimensions over the volume, performing the dot product between the kernel and input at each step. 3D convolution is commonly used in tasks such as object detection or segmentation in medical imaging.

Example:

```
from keras.layers import Conv3D

model = Sequential()
model.add(Conv3D(filters=32, kernel_size=(3, 3, 3), activation='relu',
    input_shape=(32, 32, 32, 1)))
```

In the above example, we define a 3D convolution layer with 32 filters and kernel size of (3, 3, 3). The input shape is (32, 32, 32, 1), indicating a volumetric data with dimensions of 32x32x32 and 1 input channel.

In summary, the choice between 1D, 2D, or 3D convolution depends on the input data type. 1D convolution for sequential data, 2D convolution for image data, and 3D convolution for volumetric data.

3.11   How do you use pre-trained word embeddings, such as Word2Vec or GloVe, in a Keras model?

Pre-trained word embeddings, such as Word2Vec or GloVe, can be used in a Keras model to capture the semantic meaning of words and improve the performance of natural language processing (NLP) tasks, such as sentiment analysis, question answering, and text classification.

To use pre-trained word embeddings in a Keras model, you need to follow these steps:

1. Load the pre-trained word embeddings You can use the pre-trained word embeddings provided by the authors or train your own embeddings using a large corpus of text. In Keras, you can load the pre-trained embeddings using the 'load_word2vec_format' function from the gensim library for Word2Vec embeddings or using the 'GloVe' class from the 'keras.preprocessing.text' module for GloVe embeddings. Here is an example of loading the Word2Vec embeddings:

```
import gensim

# Load pre-trained Word2Vec embeddings
word2vec_model = gensim.models.KeyedVectors.load_word2vec_format('path/to/
    word2vec.bin', binary=True)
```

Note that the 'binary' flag is set to 'True' if the model is saved in binary format.

2. Create a word index You need to create a word index that maps each word in the vocabulary to a unique integer index. In Keras, you can use the 'Tokenizer' class from the 'keras.preprocessing.text' module to create a word index. Here is an example of creating a word index:

```
from keras.preprocessing.text import Tokenizer

# Create a tokenizer
tokenizer = Tokenizer()

# Fit the tokenizer on the text corpus
tokenizer.fit_on_texts(texts)

# Create a word index
word_index = tokenizer.word_index
```

Note that the 'texts' is a list of strings, where each string represents a document or sentence in the corpus.

3. Create an embedding matrix You need to create an embedding matrix that contains the embedding vectors for each word in the word index. In Keras, you can create an embedding matrix using the 'create_embedding_matrix' function. Here is an example of creating an embedding matrix:

```
import numpy as np

# Define the embedding dimension
EMBEDDING_DIM = 300

# Create an embedding matrix
```

```
num_words = len(word_index) + 1
embedding_matrix = np.zeros((num_words, EMBEDDING_DIM))
for word, i in word_index.items():
    if word in word2vec_model:
        embedding_matrix[i] = word2vec_model[word]
```

Note that the 'num_words' is set to the number of unique words in the word index plus one, since the word index starts from 1 instead of 0.

4. Define a Keras model You need to define a Keras model that includes an embedding layer that uses the pre-trained embeddings. In Keras, you can define an embedding layer using the 'Embedding' class from the 'keras.layers.embeddings' module. Here is an example of defining a Keras model:

```
from keras.models import Sequential
from keras.layers import Embedding, Flatten, Dense

# Define the model architecture
model = Sequential()
model.add(Embedding(num_words, EMBEDDING_DIM, weights=[embedding_matrix],
    input_length=MAX_SEQUENCE_LENGTH, trainable=False))
model.add(Flatten())
model.add(Dense(1, activation='sigmoid'))

# Compile the model
model.compile(optimizer='adam', loss='binary_crossentropy', metrics=['acc'])
```

Note that the 'num_words' is set to the number of unique words in the word index plus one, the 'EMBEDDING_DIM' is set to the same dimension as the pre-trained embeddings, and the 'trainable' flag is set to 'False' to prevent the embeddings from being updated during training.

5. Train the Keras model You can train the Keras model using the 'fit' function and evaluate its performance on a held-out test set. Here is an example of training the Keras model:

```
# Train the model
model.fit(x_train, y_train, validation_data=(x_test, y_test), epochs=10,
    batch_size=64)

# Evaluate the model
loss, acc = model.evaluate(x_test, y_test)
print('Test accuracy:', acc)
```

Note that the 'x_train' and 'y_train' are the training inputs and labels, and the 'x_test' and 'y_test' are the test inputs and labels. The 'epochs' and 'batch_size' are hyperparameters that control the number of iterations and size of batches for training.

3.12 What is the purpose of a custom layer in Keras, and how do you create one?

Keras provides a number of built-in layers that can be used to construct neural networks for a variety of tasks. However, in some cases, the problem that we are trying to solve may require a layer with a different type of behavior than what is available in the standard Keras layers. This is where a custom layer comes in handy.

A custom layer in Keras allows us to define a layer with a specific behavior that meets our requirements, and then integrate that layer into our neural network model. The custom layer could implement a unique type of activation function, use a specific initialization scheme for its weights, or incorporate some external data during the forward pass.

To create a custom layer in Keras, you have to define your layer class by inheriting from Keras base Layer class. You need to implement the following three methods: - '__init__(self, args)': Initializing the layer, such as defining the layer's weights or parameters. - 'build(self, input_shape)': This method is called once at the beginning to build the layer model. It creates the required state of the layer using input shapes, like weights. - 'call(self, x)': This method executes the forward computation of the layer.

Here is an example that demonstrates how to create a custom layer that concatenates the input tensor with a trainable vector:

```
from tensorflow.keras.layers import Layer
import tensorflow.keras.backend as K

class CustomLayer(Layer):
    def __init__(self, output_dim, **kwargs):
        self.output_dim = output_dim
        super().__init__(**kwargs)

    def build(self, input_shape):
        self.kernel = self.add_weight(name='kernel',
                                      shape=(self.output_dim,),
                                      initializer='uniform',
                                      trainable=True)
        super().build(input_shape)

    def call(self, x):
        return K.concatenate([x, self.kernel * K.ones_like(x)])

    def compute_output_shape(self, input_shape):
        return input_shape[0], input_shape[1] + self.output_dim
```

The above code defines a custom layer named 'CustomLayer' that concatenates the input tensor with a trainable weight vector 'kernel'. The 'build' method initializes the 'kernel' vector with a uniform distribution and is called only once when the layer is built in the model. The 'call' method defines the forward pass for the layer, using the 'K.concatenate' method to concatenate the input tensor with the 'kernel' vector.

Overall, custom layers are an important tool in Keras for building deep learning models that can solve specific and unique problems.

3.13   How do you perform cross-validation in Keras to assess the performance of your model?

Cross-validation is a popular statistical method used to evaluate machine learning models. By performing cross-validation, you can estimate how well your model is likely to perform on unseen data, and you can also compare the performance of different models.

In Keras, there are several ways to perform cross-validation. One common approach is to use the 'KFold' function from the 'sklearn' library.

Here's an example of how to use 'KFold' with Keras:

```
from sklearn.model_selection import KFold

# Define the number of folds for cross-validation
num_folds = 5

# Initialize the KFold object
kfold = KFold(n_splits=num_folds, shuffle=True)

# Loop through the folds
for fold_num, (train_indices, val_indices) in enumerate(kfold.split(X=train_data
    )):
    # Split the training and validation data
    X_train = train_data[train_indices]
    y_train = train_labels[train_indices]
    X_val = train_data[val_indices]
    y_val = train_labels[val_indices]

    # Define your model architecture
    model = Sequential()
    # ...

    # Compile the model
```

```
model.compile(optimizer='adam', loss='binary_crossentropy', metrics=['
  accuracy'])

# Train the model on the current fold
model.fit(X_train, y_train, validation_data=(X_val, y_val), epochs=10,
  batch_size=32)

# Evaluate the model on the validation set
scores = model.evaluate(X_val, y_val, verbose=0)
print(f"Fold␣{fold_num}:␣Validation␣loss:␣{scores[0]},␣Validation␣accuracy:␣
  {scores[1]}")
```

In this example, we first define the number of folds we want to use
for cross-validation (in this case, 5). We then initialize the 'KFold'
object with 'n_splits=num_folds' and 'shuffle=True'.

Next, we loop through each fold using 'enumerate(kfold.split(X=train_data))'.
For each fold, we split the training and validation data using the in-
dices provided by 'kfold.split()'. We then define our model architecture, compile the model, and train it on the current fold. Finally, we
evaluate the model on the validation set using 'model.evaluate()'.

Note that in this example, we're printing the validation loss and accuracy for each fold. At the end of the cross-validation process, you
could average these scores across all the folds to get a single estimate
of your model's performance.

Keep in mind that cross-validation can be computationally expensive,
especially if you have a large dataset or a complex model. If you're
training your model on a GPU, you may need to adjust the batch
size to avoid running out of memory. Additionally, you may want to
consider using a stratified version of 'KFold' if you have an imbalanced
dataset.

3.14   What is the purpose of a generator in Keras, and how can you create a custom generator for your dataset?

In Keras, a generator is a way to load and preprocess data on the fly
while training a model. Rather than loading all the data into memory
at once, which can be memory-intensive and slow down training, a
generator allows you to load and preprocess data in batches during

the training process. This can be particularly useful when working with large datasets that cannot fit into memory at once.

A generator function in Keras should take no arguments and return a tuple (input, target). The input and target can be Numpy arrays or a list of Numpy arrays. The length of the input and target array should be the same, and it corresponds to the number of samples in a given batch.

Here's an example of a simple generator that loads data from a directory of image files and applies some basic preprocessing:

```
import numpy as np
from keras.preprocessing.image import ImageDataGenerator

def custom_generator(directory, batch_size):
    data_gen = ImageDataGenerator(rescale=1./255)
    data_flow = data_gen.flow_from_directory(directory, target_size=(224, 224),
                                            batch_size=batch_size, class_mode=
    'binary')
    while True:
        input_batch, target_batch = data_flow.next()
        yield input_batch, target_batch
```

In this case, the 'ImageDataGenerator' class applies rescaling to the pixel values of the images. The 'flow_from_directory' method of this class generates batches of preprocessed images from a given directory of image files. The generator function creates an infinite loop using the 'while True:' statement, and yields an input batch and a target batch at each iteration using the 'next()' method of the 'data_flow' generator object.

To use this generator in training a Keras model, you simply pass the 'custom_generator' function to the 'fit_generator' method of your model instance. For example:

```
model.fit_generator(custom_generator('data/train', batch_size=32),
                    steps_per_epoch=1000, epochs=10)
```

Here, 'steps_per_epoch' is the number of batches to yield at each epoch of model training. When using a custom generator, the number of steps per epoch should be set to the number of training samples divided by the batch size.

Overall, using a generator in Keras is a powerful tool for loading and processing data on the fly, and it can be useful for working with large datasets that cannot fit into memory at once. Creating a custom generator is straightforward once you understand the basic structure, and it allows you to customize the preprocessing steps applied to your data before feeding it to a model.

3.15 How do you implement multi-output or multi-input models in Keras using the functional API?

The Keras functional API allows for the creation of models with multiple inputs or outputs. This allows for more complex architectures, such as models with multiple branches that converge towards a common output, or models with multiple different outputs. Here are the steps to create a multi-input or multi-output model using the functional API:

1. Import the necessary modules:

```
from keras.layers import Input, Dense, Concatenate
from keras.models import Model
```

2. Define the input layers by instantiating the 'Input' class, which creates a Keras tensor:

```
input_1 = Input(shape=(input_dim_1,))
input_2 = Input(shape=(input_dim_2,))
```

Each input should be given a unique name.

3. Define the model's layers as standalone objects, and then call them on the input tensors:

```
dense_1 = Dense(hidden_dim_1, activation='relu')
dense_2 = Dense(hidden_dim_2, activation='relu')
dense_3 = Dense(output_dim, activation='softmax')

hidden_1 = dense_1(input_1)
hidden_2 = dense_2(input_2)
merged = Concatenate()([hidden_1, hidden_2])
outputs = dense_3(merged)
```

Note that 'Concatenate' is used to merge the outputs from the two hidden layers. Also, 'output_dim' corresponds to the number of classes in our classification problem.

4. Define the model using the input tensors as inputs and the output tensors as outputs:

```
model = Model(inputs=[input_1, input_2], outputs=outputs)
```

Now, we can compile and train the model, as we would do for any other Keras model. The 'fit' function expects a list of input arrays, one for each input, and yields a list of output arrays, one for each output.

Here is an example of a multi-output model, which predicts both the species and the size of flowers based on their images and metadata:

```
input_img = Input(shape=(img_width, img_height, 3), name='img_input')
input_meta = Input(shape=(metadata_dim,), name='meta_input')

x = Conv2D(32, (3,3), activation='relu')(input_img)
x = MaxPooling2D()(x)
x = Conv2D(64, (3,3), activation='relu')(x)
x = MaxPooling2D()(x)
x = Conv2D(128, (3,3), activation='relu')(x)
x = MaxPooling2D()(x)
x = Flatten()(x)
x = Dense(128, activation='relu')(x)

merged = Concatenate()([x, input_meta])

out_species = Dense(num_species, activation='softmax', name='species_output')(x)
out_size = Dense(num_sizes, activation='softmax', name='size_output')(merged)

model = Model(inputs=[input_img, input_meta], outputs=[out_species, out_size])

model.compile(optimizer='adam', loss='categorical_crossentropy', metrics=['
    accuracy'])

model.fit([train_images, train_metadata], [train_species, train_sizes], epochs
    =10, batch_size=32, validation_data=([val_images, val_metadata], [
    val_species, val_sizes]))
```

In this example, 'Conv2D' and 'MaxPooling2D' layers are used to extract features from the input images, and the metadata is concatenated with the flattened feature map. The final model has two outputs: 'out_species' and 'out_size'.

3.16 Can you explain the concept of a residual connection, and how it can be implemented in Keras?

Residual connections are an essential component of modern deep learning architectures, and they can significantly improve model performance by making it easier for the model to propagate gradients and learn complex relationships between inputs and outputs.

In essence, a residual connection allows a model to "skip" over certain layers of its architecture, bypassing them entirely and allowing the input to flow directly through to a later layer. This is accomplished by adding the original input to the output of some intermediate layer, effectively creating a "shortcut" that can help the model circumvent any barriers to learning that might arise in the intervening layers.

The implementation of residual connections in Keras is straightforward, and there are several ways to do it depending on the specific architecture of your model. One common approach is to use the 'Add' layer from Keras' functional API to combine the output of a given layer with its input, as follows:

```
from tensorflow.keras.layers import Input, Dense, Add
from tensorflow.keras.models import Model

inputs = Input(shape=(input_dim,))
x = Dense(units=64, activation='relu')(inputs)
y = Dense(units=64, activation='relu')(x)
z = Dense(units=output_dim, activation='softmax')(y)
z = Add()([z, inputs]) # residual connection
model = Model(inputs=inputs, outputs=z)
```

In this example, we define a simple feedforward neural network with two hidden layers and an output layer, and we add a residual connection between the output layer ('z') and the input layer ('inputs'). The 'Add' layer simply sums its two input tensors element-wise, allowing the output of the 'z' layer to be combined with the original input to produce the final output of the model.

It's worth noting that residual connections are most commonly used in models that employ many layers, such as convolutional neural networks (CNNs) or residual networks (ResNets), where the gradient signal can easily become diluted or lost altogether as it propagates through numerous nonlinear transformations. By allowing information to flow directly from the input to the final output, residual connections help mitigate this problem and make it easier for the model to learn complex relationships between inputs and outputs.

3.17 What are the differences between stateful and stateless RNNs in Keras, and when should you use each?

Recurrent Neural Networks (RNNs) are a type of neural network that can take into account the sequential nature of data, and are extensively used for sequence prediction and text generation tasks. There are two major classes of RNNs: stateful and stateless, and each has its advantages and disadvantages depending on the nature of the task at hand.

Stateless RNNs: In a stateless RNN, the model treats each input sequence as an independent entity, and does not take into account any information from previous sequences. This means that at the start of each input sequence, the hidden state of the RNN is initialized to zero. Stateless RNNs are very useful when you have relatively short input sequences, and the information from previous sequences does not have a significant impact on the prediction of the current sequence. They are also generally faster to train than their stateful counterparts, as there is no need to maintain the state from previous sequences.

Stateful RNNs: In a stateful RNN, the model takes the output of the previous input sequence as input to the current input sequence. This means that the hidden state of the RNN is carried over from one sequence to another, which allows the model to maintain contextual information across sequences. Stateful RNNs are generally used when the data is highly sequential and contextual, and the output of the previous sequence is highly correlated with the output of the current sequence, as is the case with speech recognition or language modelling. Since stateful RNNs maintain the state from previous sequences, they require more memory to train and may take longer to converge than stateless RNNs.

In general, the choice between stateful and stateless RNNs depends on the length of input sequences, the amount of contextual information required, and the correlation between consecutive sequences. If the input sequences are long and highly correlated, then stateful RNNs may be more appropriate. Conversely, if the input sequences are short or uncorrelated, then stateless RNNs may be more appropriate.

3.18   How do you visualize the architecture and training progress of a Keras model?

There are several ways to visualize the architecture and training progress of a Keras model. Here are some commonly used methods:

1. Model Visualization - To visualize the architecture of a Keras model, we can use the 'plot_model' function from the 'keras.utils.vis_utils' module. This function generates a plot of the model architecture in a graphical format. For example:

```
from keras.utils.vis_utils import plot_model
plot_model(model, to_file='model.png', show_shapes=True, show_layer_names=True)
```

This will create a PNG image of the model architecture with shapes and layer names.

2. Training Visualization - To visualize the training progress of a Keras model, we can plot the training history using the 'matplotlib' library. This allows us to see how the training and validation loss and accuracy change over time. For example:

```
import matplotlib.pyplot as plt

# plot training and validation loss
plt.plot(history.history['loss'])
plt.plot(history.history['val_loss'])
plt.title('Model Loss')
plt.ylabel('Loss')
plt.xlabel('Epoch')
plt.legend(['Training', 'Validation'], loc='upper right')
plt.show()

# plot training and validation accuracy
plt.plot(history.history['acc'])
plt.plot(history.history['val_acc'])
plt.title('Model Accuracy')
plt.ylabel('Accuracy')
plt.xlabel('Epoch')
plt.legend(['Training', 'Validation'], loc='lower right')
plt.show()
```

3. TensorBoard - TensorBoard is a tool in TensorFlow that allows us to visualize various aspects of our model, including the architecture and training progress. We can use the 'TensorBoard' callback in Keras to write log files that can be visualized using TensorBoard. For example:

```
from keras.callbacks import TensorBoard
tensorboard = TensorBoard(log_dir='logs/{}'.format(time()))

model.fit(X_train, Y_train, validation_split=0.2, epochs=50, batch_size=32,
    callbacks=[tensorboard])
```

This code will log the relevant training and validation metrics to a directory named "logs" during training. Once training is complete, we can launch TensorBoard using the following command 'tensorboard –logdir=logs/' and access the visualization results in a web browser (http://localhost:6006/).

3.19   What are some strategies for handling overfitting and underfitting when using convolutional neural networks (CNNs) in Keras?

Overfitting and underfitting are common challenges when training convolutional neural networks (CNNs) in Keras. Overfitting occurs when the model performs well on the training data but poorly on the validation or test data, whereas underfitting occurs when the model is too simplistic and performs poorly on both the training and validation data. Here are some strategies for handling overfitting and underfitting in CNNs:

1. Regularization: Regularization is a common technique used to prevent overfitting by introducing additional constraints to the model parameters, such as L1, L2, or dropout regularization. L1 and L2 regularization add a penalty term to the loss function that forces the model to use smaller weights, while dropout randomly drops out neurons during training to prevent co-adaptation offeatures.

2. Early stopping: Early stopping is a technique that stops the training process when the performance on the validation data starts to degrade. This ensures that the model doesn't overfit to the training data and generalizes well to new data'.

3. Data augmentation: Data augmentation is a technique used to generate more training data by applying random transformations, such as flips, rotations, and zooms, to the existing data. This helps

the model to generalize better to new data and reduces overfitting.

4. Reduce model complexity: Reducing the complexity of the model by decreasing the number of layers, filters, or neurons can help prevent overfitting. Also, increasing the depth or width of the network can help address underfitting.

5. Tuning hyperparameters: Hyperparameters, such as learning rate, batch size, and optimizer, can greatly affect the performance of the model. Tuning these hyperparameters can help prevent both overfitting and underfitting and improve model performance.

For example, a CNN model that is prone to overfitting can be regularized using dropout regularization or early stopping, while a model that is underfitting can be improved by adding more layers or filters or increasing the number of neurons in each layer. Similarly, reducing model complexity, augmenting data or tuning hyperparameters can also be effective strategies to handle overfitting and underfitting in CNNs.

3.20 Can you explain the difference between one-shot learning and few-shot learning, and how Keras can be used for these tasks?

One-shot learning and few-shot learning are both techniques in deep learning and machine learning that are used to handle situations where there is a scarcity of labeled data. The difference between these two methods lies in the amount of labeled data required to train a model.

One-shot learning refers to a classification problem that requires only one labeled example per class to build a model. This type of learning is interesting as it simulates a situation where we need to recognize an object or pattern we have only seen once or a few times.

Few-shot learning goes a step further from one-shot learning, and it refers to classification tasks that require only very few training examples per class. In typical applications, a "few shot" means a few tens of training samples, which is considerably smaller than the hundreds or thousands of examples that are traditionally required by deep learning algorithms.

In recent years, Keras has been seen as an easy-to-use library for implementing one-shot and few-shot learning methods. Specifically, Keras provides a wide range of deep learning models and techniques, including Convolutional Neural Networks (CNNs), which can be used to build one-shot and few-shot learning models.

Keras supports one-shot and few-shot learning through the help of transfer learning, which allows a pre-trained model to learn from a limited set of data by adapting to the new target domain. With transfer learning, a deep CNN model, pre-trained on a large image classification dataset such as ImageNet, can be fine-tuned to achieve high accuracy on a few-shot or one-shot learning task.

Aside from transfer learning, Keras also provides several few-shot learning techniques such as Matching Networks, Prototypical Networks, and Siamese Networks. These networks can learn a metric space for accurate comparison and classification even when labeled data is scarce.

In summary, both one-shot and few-shot learning are powerful techniques in machine learning and deep learning that allow us to train models on a limited amount of labeled data. Keras provides several techniques to implement these methods, and it is an excellent choice for building one-shot and few-shot learning models.

Chapter 4

Advanced

4.1 Can you explain the concept of attention mechanisms in neural networks, and how they can be implemented in Keras?

Attention mechanisms are a set of techniques used in neural networks to improve their ability to focus on the most relevant parts of an input sequence. In other words, attention mechanisms allow a model to selectively attend to specific parts of the input to make predictions or generate outputs. This is particularly useful in tasks that involve working with sequential data, such as machine translation, speech recognition, and image captioning.

The basic idea behind attention mechanisms is to incorporate a mechanism that learns to assign different weights to different parts of the input data. These weights are then used to compute a weighted sum of the input sequence, where the weights are based on how relevant each element of the sequence is to the current prediction or output.

In Keras, you can implement attention mechanisms using the 'attention' layer in the 'addons' package. Here's an example of how to use the 'attention' layer in a Keras model:

```
from keras.layers import Input, LSTM, Dense, attention
from keras.models import Model

# Define the input sequence
inputs = Input(shape=(None, input_dim))

# Add an LSTM layer with return sequences to get the output sequence
lstm_out = LSTM(units, return_sequences=True)(inputs)

# Add an attention layer to compute the attention weights
attention_weights = attention.Attention()([lstm_out, lstm_out])

# Use the attention weights to compute a weighted sum of the input sequence
context_vector = keras.layers.Dot(axes=1)([attention_weights, lstm_out])

# Concatenate the output of the attention layer with the context vector
output = keras.layers.concatenate([context_vector, lstm_out])

# Add a dense layer and softmax activation for the final predictions
output = keras.layers.Dense(units=output_dim, activation='softmax')(output)

# Create the model
model = Model(inputs=inputs, outputs=output)
```

In this example, we first define the input sequence and add an LSTM layer with 'return_sequences=True' to get the output sequence. We then add an 'attention' layer to compute the attention weights based on the LSTM output, and use these weights to compute a weighted sum of the LSTM output. Finally, we concatenate the output of the attention layer with the context vector and add a dense layer and softmax activation for the final predictions.

Note that this is just one example of how to implement attention mechanisms in Keras, and there are many variations and techniques to customize the implementation for different tasks and models.

4.2   What are the key differences between GRU and LSTM layers in Keras, and when might you choose one over the other?

GRU (Gated Recurrent Unit) and LSTM (Long Short-Term Memory) are both popular choices for recurrent layers in deep learning models that deal with sequences, such as time series forecasting or natural language processing. While they have some similarities, they differ in the way they handle information flow and memory management.

The main difference between GRU and LSTM is the number of gates they use to control the flow of information. GRU has two gates (reset and update) while LSTM has three (input, output, and forget). These gates act as filters that decide how much of the incoming data to keep, discard, or update in the memory cell.

In terms of training speed and computational efficiency, GRU is generally faster than LSTM because it has fewer parameters to learn. However, LSTMs have proven to be more effective in capturing long-term dependencies in sequences and dealing with the vanishing gradient problem.

When it comes to choosing between GRU and LSTM, it depends on the specific problem you are trying to solve and the nature of the data you are working with. Here are some general guidelines:

1. If your data is relatively simple and short-term dependencies are more important, you may choose GRU for its simplicity and speed.

2. If your data is more complex and long-term dependencies are critical, LSTM is usually a better choice.

3. If you're not sure, you can experiment with both models and compare their performances on your validation/test dataset.

4. In some cases, a combination of both GRU and LSTM layers can be used to achieve better results, as each type of layer has its own strengths.

For example, in language modeling tasks like sequence to sequence translation, LSTM has been shown to perform better than GRU. However, in tasks that involve shorter sequences, such as speech recognition, GRU may be a more efficient choice.

In summary, while GRU and LSTM are similar in some ways, they have distinct differences that can impact the performance of the model. The choice of which one to use depends on the specific problem at hand and the nature of the data.

4.3   How do you implement custom loss functions and custom metrics in Keras, and when would you need to do so?

In Keras, you can implement custom loss functions and custom metrics by defining them as functions using the backend functions provided by Keras.

A custom loss function can be defined by creating a function that takes in two arguments - y_true (the ground truth values) and y_pred (the predicted values) - and returns a scalar value representing the loss. For example, let's say you want to implement a custom loss function called "weighted_binary_crossentropy" that calculates binary cross-entropy with a weighted penalty for misclassifying positive and negative samples, you could define it as follows:

```
import keras.backend as K

def weighted_binary_crossentropy(y_true, y_pred):
    # Set class weights as an example
    class_weight_0 = 0.2
    class_weight_1 = 0.8

    # Calculate binary crossentropy
    bce = K.binary_crossentropy(y_true, y_pred)

    # Apply weights
    weighted_bce = class_weight_0*(1-y_true)*K.log(1-y_pred) +
                   class_weight_1*(y_true)*K.log(y_pred)

    return -K.mean(weighted_bce)
```

To use this custom loss function, you would simply pass its name to the 'compile()' method of your Keras model:

```
model.compile(optimizer='adam',
              loss=weighted_binary_crossentropy)
```

Similarly, a custom metric can be defined by creating a function that takes in two arguments - y_true and y_pred - and returns a scalar value representing the metric. For example, let's say you want to implement a custom metric called "f1_score" that calculates the F1 score of a binary classification problem, you could define it as follows:

```
def f1_score(y_true, y_pred):
    # Calculate true positives, false positives, and false negatives
    tp = K.sum(K.round(K.clip(y_true * y_pred, 0, 1)))
    fp = K.sum(K.round(K.clip(y_pred - y_true, 0, 1)))
    fn = K.sum(K.round(K.clip(y_true - y_pred, 0, 1)))

    # Calculate precision and recall
```

```
p = tp / (tp + fp + K.epsilon())
r = tp / (tp + fn + K.epsilon())

# Calculate F1 score
f1 = 2*(p*r) / (p+r+K.epsilon())

return f1
```

To use this custom metric, you would pass its name to the 'compile()' method of your Keras model, just as you would with a built-in metric:

```
model.compile(optimizer='adam',
              loss='binary_crossentropy',
              metrics=[f1_score])
```

You might need to implement custom loss functions or custom metrics when working with complex machine learning problems where the built-in Keras functionalities may not be sufficient. For example, you might want to implement a custom loss function or metric when working with imbalanced datasets, or when you are working on a problem where the built-in functionality does not provide an adequate solution. In general, it is a good idea to use built-in loss functions and metrics whenever possible, as they are generally well optimized and well documented. However, when they are not adequate, Keras provides the flexibility of implementing custom functions to suit your needs.

4.4 Can you describe the process of creating an end-to-end pipeline for a deep learning project using Keras?

The process of creating an end-to-end pipeline for a deep learning project using Keras can be divided into the following main steps:

1. Data Preparation: The first step in building an end-to-end pipeline for a deep learning project is to prepare the data. This involves gathering and cleaning the data, and then splitting it into training, validation, and testing sets. In Keras, we can use the 'ImageDataGenerator' class to load and preprocess image data, while for other types of data, we can use 'numpy' arrays or Pandas dataframes for handling data.

2. Model Definition: The second step in building an end-to-end

pipeline is to define the architecture of the model we want to train. Keras provides a simple way to define and compile deep learning models using the 'Sequential' or functional API. We define the input layer, hidden layers, and output layer, and choose the appropriate activation functions and loss functions based on the problem were trying to solve.

3. Model Training: Next, we train the model using the training and validation data. Keras provides a variety of optimization algorithms, such as Stochastic Gradient Descent (SGD) or Adam, that make the training process easier. We compile the model using the 'compile' method and then train the model using the 'fit' method. We can also use various callbacks to monitor the training process and stop training once a certain criteria has been met.

4. Model Evaluation: Once weve trained the model, we evaluate its performance on the testing dataset. Using the 'evaluate' method, we can compute various metrics like accuracy, precision, recall, and F1 score.

5. Model Deployment: Finally, we can deploy the trained model to make predictions on new data. This can be done either by using the 'predict' method directly in Python code or by building an API for accessing the model through a website or mobile app.

To summarize, the process of creating an end-to-end pipeline for a deep learning project using Keras involves data preparation, model definition, model training, model evaluation, and model deployment. Keras provides a simple and intuitive API for each step of the process, making it easier to build and deploy deep learning models even for those with limited experience.

4.5 What are some advanced techniques for data augmentation in Keras, and how do they help improve model performance?

Data augmentation is a technique used to artificially expand the size of a dataset by applying various transformations on existing data such as rotations, zooms, translations, flips, and shifts. In Keras, data augmentation can be easily accomplished using the 'ImageDataGenerator' class. Here are some advanced techniques for data augmentation in Keras:

1. **Random erasing:** This method involves randomly removing rectangular patches from an image. It helps to make the model more robust to occlusions and missing information in the images.

2. **Cutout:** Cutout is a similar technique to random erasing, except instead of removing rectangular patches from an image, it masks out square regions. Cutout can be an effective regularization technique, as it encourages the model to learn more robust features.

3. **Mixup:** Mixup is a data augmentation technique where two images are combined by taking weighted averages of their pixel values and labels. The idea is to regularize the model by forcing it to learn from linear combinations of examples, rather than just memorizing individual examples.

4. **Style transfer:** Style transfer is a technique where the style of one image is transferred onto another image. It can be used in data augmentation by randomly selecting a style image, and then transferring that style onto a new image. This can help to create more diverse training examples, which can improve the model's ability to generalize to new data.

5. **GAN-based augmentation:** GAN stands for Generative Adversarial Network, a type of deep learning architecture. GAN-based data augmentation involves training a GAN to generate new synthetic images that are similar to the training examples. This can be an effective way to generate more diverse training data, which can help to mitigate overfitting.

These advanced data augmentation techniques can help to improve model performance by increasing the diversity of the training set. By introducing more variation into the training data, the model is better able to generalize to new data that it has not seen before. This can lead to better performance on test data, and can help to reduce overfitting.

4.6 How do you parallelize the training of a Keras model using multiple GPUs, and what are the main challenges involved?

Parallelizing the training of a Keras model using multiple GPUs can significantly speed up the training process and reduce the time required to train a deep learning model. There are several ways to parallelize the training process of a Keras model, and each method has its own benefits and challenges. Here, I will explain two popular methods for parallelizing training in Keras with multiple GPUs: data parallelism and model parallelism.

Data Parallelism:

Data parallelism involves training the same model on multiple GPUs with different parts of the training data. In this method, each GPU receives a batch of training data and computes the gradients independently. The gradients are then combined and averaged across all GPUs, and the weights of the model are updated accordingly.

Here are the steps for implementing data parallelism in Keras:

- 1. Split the training data into equal parts, with each part assigned to a separate GPU.

- 2. Replicate the model across all GPUs.

- 3. Define a custom Keras callback to collect the gradients from all GPUs.

- 4. During each iteration of training, pass a batch of training data to each GPU and compute the gradients independently.

- 5. Use the custom callback to collect the gradients from all GPUs and average them.

- 6. Use the averaged gradients to update the weights of the model.

One of the main challenges of data parallelism is the communication overhead between GPUs. Since the gradients need to be transferred between GPUs during each iteration, the speed of the network connection between the GPUs can significantly affect the performance of the model.

Model Parallelism:

Model parallelism involves dividing the model across multiple GPUs, with each GPU responsible for computing a specific part of the model. In this method, each GPU receives a portion of the input data, and the computations are performed in parallel across all GPUs. The output from each GPU is then combined to produce the final output.

Here are the steps for implementing model parallelism in Keras:

- 1. Split various layers of the model across different GPUs.

- 2. Define a custom Keras callback to pass the inputs through the multiple model parts and gather the outputs.

- 3. During each iteration of training, pass a batch of training data to each GPU.

- 4. Use the custom callback to compute the output for each GPU and combine them to produce the final output.

- 5. Use the combined output to compute the loss and update the weights of the model.

One of the main challenges of model parallelism is the design of the model itself. The model needs to be designed to allow for the division of layers across multiple GPUs, and not all models are suitable for

this approach.   Additionally, maintaining consistency between the
different parts of the model can be challenging.

In summary, parallelizing the training of a Keras model using multiple
GPUs can significantly reduce the training time. However, different
strategies, such as data parallelism and model parallelism, have their
own benefits and challenges.

4.7   What is the role of skip connections in neural networks, and how do you implement them using the Keras functional API?

Skip connections, also known as residual connections, are connections
that go around one or more layers in a neural network. They are used
in deep neural networks to address the vanishing gradient problem,
which can occur when the gradients become too small during backpropagation and prevent the network from learning well.

By adding skip connections, information can flow more easily through
the network, making it easier for the network to learn useful representations of the input data. Rather than relying on each layer to learn
everything about the input data, skip connections enable the network
to learn a more hierarchical representation of the data, where lower-
level features are learned independently and then combined in later
layers.

In the Keras functional API, skip connections can be implemented
by concatenating the output of one layer with the output of another
layer that is further down the network. Here's an example:

```
from tensorflow.keras.layers import Input, Conv2D, Concatenate

# Define input shape
input_shape = (100, 100, 3)

# Define input tensor
inputs = Input(shape=input_shape)

# Define first convolutional block
x1 = Conv2D(32, (3,3), activation='relu', padding='same')(inputs)
x1 = Conv2D(32, (3,3), activation='relu', padding='same')(x1)

# Define second convolutional block with skip connection
x2 = Conv2D(64, (3,3), activation='relu', padding='same')(x1)
```

```
x2 = Conv2D(64, (3,3), activation='relu', padding='same')(x2)
x2 = Concatenate()([x2, x1]) # concatenate skip connection here

# Define third convolutional block
x3 = Conv2D(128, (3,3), activation='relu', padding='same')(x2)
x3 = Conv2D(128, (3,3), activation='relu', padding='same')(x3)

# Define output layer
outputs = Conv2D(1, (1,1), activation='sigmoid')(x3)

# Create model
model = Model(inputs=inputs, outputs=outputs)
```

In this example, we define an input tensor with shape (100, 100, 3) and create a neural network with three convolutional blocks. The second block includes a skip connection, where the output of the first convolutional block is concatenated with the output of the second convolutional block. This concatenated tensor is then passed to the third convolutional block.

By using skip connections, we can reduce the impact of vanishing gradients and improve the overall performance of the neural network.

4.8 Can you explain the concept of teacher forcing in sequence-to-sequence models, and how it can be implemented in Keras?

In sequence-to-sequence (Seq2Seq) models, the output sequence is generated by predicting the next element in the sequence one at a time, based on the previously generated elements. This process is usually done using an RNN-based model, such as an LSTM or GRU. During training, the model is usually fed the true (ground truth) previous element as part of the input, and the true next element as the expected output. However, during inference (when generating new sequences), the model is not provided with the ground truth previous element and must generate it by itself.

Teacher forcing refers to the practice of training Seq2Seq models by feeding the model the true previous element as its input during training, even when generating the current sequence element that will become the input at the next step. This can be thought of as "forcing" the model to learn to predict the next element even when given imperfect previous elements, making it more robust to errors and variations.

In Keras, teacher forcing can be implemented by using the 'training' parameter of the 'tf.keras.layers.RNN()' layer. Setting 'training=True' will use the true input sequence during training, while setting it to 'False' will use the predicted output sequence as the input at the next step.

Here's an example of how to implement teacher forcing in a Seq2Seq model in Keras:

```
encoder_inputs = tf.keras.Input(shape=(None, num_encoder_tokens))
encoder = tf.keras.layers.LSTM(latent_dim, return_state=True)
encoder_outputs, state_h, state_c = encoder(encoder_inputs)
encoder_states = [state_h, state_c]

decoder_inputs = tf.keras.Input(shape=(None, num_decoder_tokens))
decoder_lstm = tf.keras.layers.LSTM(latent_dim, return_sequences=True,
    return_state=True)
decoder_outputs, _, _ = decoder_lstm(decoder_inputs, initial_state=
    encoder_states)
decoder_dense = tf.keras.layers.Dense(num_decoder_tokens, activation='softmax')
decoder_outputs = decoder_dense(decoder_outputs)

model = tf.keras.Model([encoder_inputs, decoder_inputs], decoder_outputs)

model.compile(optimizer='adam', loss='categorical_crossentropy', metrics=['
    accuracy'])

# Train model with true previous element as input (teacher forcing)
model.fit([encoder_input_data, decoder_input_data], decoder_target_data,
    batch_size=batch_size,
        epochs=epochs, validation_split=0.2)

# Inference mode (with generator). Use predicted previous element as input
encoder_model = tf.keras.Model(encoder_inputs, encoder_states)

decoder_state_input_h = tf.keras.Input(shape=(latent_dim,))
decoder_state_input_c = tf.keras.Input(shape=(latent_dim,))
decoder_states_inputs = [decoder_state_input_h, decoder_state_input_c]

decoder_outputs, state_h, state_c = decoder_lstm(
    decoder_inputs, initial_state=decoder_states_inputs)
decoder_states = [state_h, state_c]
decoder_outputs = decoder_dense(decoder_outputs)
decoder_model = tf.keras.Model(
    [decoder_inputs] + decoder_states_inputs,
    [decoder_outputs] + decoder_states)

# Generate new sequences
def generate_seq(input_seq):
    # Encode the input as state vectors.
    states_value = encoder_model.predict(input_seq)

    # Generate empty target sequence of length 1.
    target_seq = np.zeros((1, 1, num_decoder_tokens))
    # Populate the first element of target sequence with the start character.
    target_seq[0, 0, target_token_index['t']] = 1.

    # Sampling loop for a batch of sequences
```

```
# (to simplify, here we assume a batch of size 1).
stop_condition = False
generated_sequence = ''
while not stop_condition:
    # Predict the next character using the decoder model
    output_tokens, h, c = decoder_model.predict(
        [target_seq] + states_value)

    # Update the states
    states_value = [h, c]

    # Sample a token
    sampled_token_index = np.argmax(output_tokens[0, -1, :])
    sampled_char = reverse_target_char_index[sampled_token_index]
    generated_sequence += sampled_char

    # Exit condition
    if (sampled_char == 'n' or
        len(generated_sequence) > max_decoder_seq_length):
        stop_condition = True

    # Update the target sequence (using the predicted output as input)
    target_seq = np.zeros((1, 1, num_decoder_tokens))
    target_seq[0, 0, sampled_token_index] = 1.

return generated_sequence
```

In the code above, the model is trained with ground truth previous elements by passing the true input and target sequences into the 'fit()' method. In inference mode, the 'encoder_model' and 'decoder_model' are used to generate new sequences, with the predicted output sequence being fed back into the 'decoder_model' at each step. This is done until the end of the sequence is reached or a maximum sequence length is reached.

4.9 How do you deal with variable-length input sequences in Keras, particularly in the context of RNNs?

In Keras, RNNs (Recurrent Neural Networks) are a powerful class of neural networks that can naturally handle variable-length input sequences. However, there are several things that need to be considered when dealing with variable-length input sequences in Keras.

Here are some techniques to deal with variable-length input sequences in Keras, particularly in the context of RNNs:

1. Padding: One way to deal with variable-length input sequences is to pad them to a fixed length. Padding is simply adding zeros to

the shorter sequences to make them the same length as the longest
one. In Keras, we can use the 'pad_sequence()' function from the
'preprocessing.sequence' module to pad the sequences.

2. Truncation: Another way to deal with variable-length input sequences is to truncate the longer sequences to a fixed length. We
can use the 'truncate_sequences()' function from the same module
to truncate the longer sequences.

3. Masking: Masking is a technique used to tell the network to ignore
padded values during training. In Keras, we can use the 'Masking'
layer to achieve this. The 'Masking' layer takes a mask value and
masks any sequence element equal to the mask value.

4. Using the 'batch_size' argument: When training RNNs, Keras
processes input sequences in batches. We can set the 'batch_size'
argument to 'None' so that Keras can automatically handle variable-
length input sequences. However, this can result in slower training as
Keras has to allocate memory for the largest sequence in each batch.

Here is an example code snippet that demonstrates how to use these
techniques:

```
from keras.preprocessing.sequence import pad_sequences, truncate_sequences
from keras.layers import Masking, LSTM, Dense
from keras.models import Sequential

# Define the maximum sequence length
max_sequence_length = 100

# Generate variable-length input sequences
sequences = [[1, 2, 3], [4, 5, 6, 7], [8, 9]]

# Pad the sequences to a fixed length
padded_sequences = pad_sequences(sequences, maxlen=max_sequence_length, padding=
    'post', truncating='post')

# Truncate the sequences to a fixed length
truncated_sequences = truncate_sequences(sequences, maxlen=max_sequence_length,
    truncating='post')

# Create a model with a Masking layer and an LSTM layer
model = Sequential()
model.add(Masking(mask_value=0, input_shape=(max_sequence_length, )))
model.add(LSTM(32))
model.add(Dense(1, activation='sigmoid'))

# Compile the model
model.compile('adam', loss='binary_crossentropy', metrics=['accuracy'])

# Train the model with variable-length input sequences
model.fit(padded_sequences, [0, 1, 1], batch_size=None, epochs=10)
```

In this example, we generate variable-length input sequences and pad them to a fixed length using the 'pad_sequences()' function. We then create a model with a Masking layer, an LSTM layer, and a Dense layer. Finally, we train the model with the padded sequences using the 'fit()' method with 'batch_size=None'.

4.10 What is the purpose of using reinforcement learning with Keras, and how can you implement it?

The purpose of using reinforcement learning (RL) with Keras is to enable machines to learn and make decisions based on trial and error, just like humans do, by receiving rewards or punishments for their actions. The primary goal of RL is to train an agent to find the optimal or near-optimal policy to maximize the expected rewards it receives over time.

Keras is a popular deep learning framework used to build and train artificial neural networks, and it is an excellent framework for implementing RL algorithms. Reinforcement learning algorithms typically combine a deep neural network with a decision-making algorithm, such as Q-learning or policy gradients, to optimize the agent's behavior.

Implementing RL with Keras typically involves the following steps:

1. Defining the model architecture: This involves specifying the neural network layers, activations, and any other relevant parameters required for the model.

2. Defining the reward function: This involves defining the function that evaluates the agent's actions and provides a reward or punishment.

3. Defining the RL algorithm: This involves selecting and implementing an RL algorithm, such as Q-learning, policy gradients or actor-critic.

4. Training the model: This involves feeding the agent with data and letting it learn using the reward function and the RL algorithm in

an iterative process. During training, the agent learns to take the actions that result in the highest reward.

5. Evaluating the model: This involves assessing the agent's performance after training to determine whether it has achieved the desired behavior or not.

6. Deployment: This involves deploying the trained model in a real-world scenario to handle unseen situations and make autonomous decisions without human intervention.

To summarize, implementing RL with Keras enables machines to learn from their environment to make optimal decisions without the need for explicit instructions, and Keras provides the tools to build, train and evaluate RL models.

4.11   How do you fine-tune a pre-trained Keras model, and what are some best practices to consider during this process?

Fine-tuning a pre-trained Keras model involves taking a model that has already been trained on a large dataset and retraining it on a smaller dataset with a similar problem. Fine-tuning is often done to improve the performance of the pre-trained model on a specific task, and to reduce the amount of data required for training.

To fine-tune a pre-trained Keras model, there are several steps that you can follow:

1. Select a pre-trained Keras model that is relevant to your application. Examples of popular pre-trained models include VGG16, InceptionV3, ResNet, and MobileNet.

2. Freeze the layers of the pre-trained model that you do not want to retrain. This is done by setting the 'trainable' attribute of each layer to 'False'. By freezing some layers, you can leverage the pre-trained model's ability to extract high-level features while still allowing some layers to adapt to the new task.

3. Add new layers to the pre-trained model to adapt it to the new task. These layers are typically added on top of the existing layers of the pre-trained model. For example, you could add a few fully-connected layers followed by a output layer for classification.

4. Train the model on the new dataset. You can use a smaller learning rate than the pre-trained model to prevent the new layers from overwriting the pre-trained weights. Also, you can use data augmentation techniques (such as random cropping, flipping, and rotation) to increase the diversity of the training data and prevent overfitting.

5. Fine-tune the entire model (if necessary). If the performance of the model on the new task is not satisfactory, you can unfreeze some layers of the pre-trained model and continue training on the new dataset with a smaller learning rate.

When fine-tuning a pre-trained Keras model, there are several best practices to consider:

- Use a similar dataset for fine-tuning: The dataset used to fine-tune the pre-trained model should be similar to the dataset it was originally trained on.

- Use a small learning rate: Start with a small learning rate, so that the new layers do not overwrite the pre-trained weights.

- Use data augmentation techniques: Use data augmentation techniques to increase the diversity of the training data and prevent over-fitting.

- Monitor performance: Monitor the performance of the model during training to ensure that it is not overfitting on the training data.

- Unfreeze layers gradually: If the performance of the model is not satisfactory, unfreeze some layers of the pre-trained model and continue training with a smaller learning rate.

- Reuse trained weights: It is important to save the weights of the pre-trained network as they are used for transfer learning. So, use the cache_dir argument on the keras.datasets.load_data method to keep the downloaded data in storage.

In general, fine-tuning a pre-trained Keras model can save a consider-

able amount of time and resources while also achieving high accuracy
in the new task.

4.12   Can you explain the concept of adversarial training and how it can be used with Keras to improve model robustness?

Adversarial training is a technique used to improve the robustness of
machine learning models. The basic idea in adversarial training is
to introduce carefully crafted adversarial examples into the training
data. These adversarial examples are created by adding small pertur-
bations to the input data in a way that is designed to fool the model
into making incorrect predictions.

By training models on adversarial examples, we can improve their
ability to generalize to new and unseen data. This is because the
adversarial examples represent a kind of "worst-case scenario" for the
model, and by training on them we are essentially making the model
more resilient to attacks or other unexpected behavior.

In Keras, adversarial training can be implemented using a technique
called adversarial training with Keras, which is implemented in the
popular Keras Adversarial Library (KALI). The basic idea in KALI is
to define a new loss function and train the model on both the original
data and adversarial examples computed using a separate generator
network.

Here's an example of how adversarial training might be implemented
in Keras using KALI:

```
from keras.models import Sequential
from keras.layers import Dense
from keras.datasets import mnist
from keras.optimizers import Adam
from keras_adversarial import AdversarialModel, simple_gan, gan_targets

# Load data
(X_train, y_train), (X_test, y_test) = mnist.load_data()

# Preprocess data
X_train = X_train.astype('float32') / 255.
X_test = X_test.astype('float32') / 255.

# Define generator and discriminator models
```

```
generator = Sequential([Dense(128, input_shape=(100,), activation='relu'),
                        Dense(28*28, activation='sigmoid')])
discriminator = Sequential([Dense(128, input_shape=(28*28,), activation='relu'),
                        Dense(1, activation='sigmoid')])
gan = simple_gan(generator, discriminator, normal_latent_sampling((100,)))

# Define the adversarial model
adversarial_model = AdversarialModel(base_model=gan,
                                     player_params=[generator.trainable_weights,
                                                    discriminator.
    trainable_weights])

# Compile the adversarial model
adversarial_model.compile(optimizer=Adam(1e-4, decay=1e-4),
                        loss=gan_targets)

# Train the adversarial model
adversarial_model.fit(X_train, gan_targets(X_train.shape[0]), epochs=20,
    batch_size=32)
```

This code defines a generator model and a discriminator model for training a GAN (Generative Adversarial Network) on the MNIST dataset. The adversarial model is created by passing both the generator and discriminator to the 'adversarial_model' function. The adversarial loss function is defined in the 'gan_targets' function, which computes the target values for the generator and discriminator during training.

By training the adversarial model on both the original MNIST data and adversarial examples generated by the generator network, we can improve the robustness of the model and make it less susceptible to attacks.

4.13 What are some key differences between autoencoders and variational autoencoders, and how can they be implemented in Keras?

Autoencoders and Variational Autoencoders (VAE) are both neural network models with the capability of encoding, decoding, and generating data. However, they have some fundamental differences in their structures and applications.

Autoencoders learn an efficient representation of the input data by compressing the data into a low-dimensional feature vector (encoder) and then reconstructing the original data from that vector (decoder). Autoencoders can be seen as a form of unsupervised learning, where the model learns to compress data without any explicit labels or targets. The goal of an autoencoder is to minimize the difference between the input data and the reconstructed output.

On the other hand, VAEs are a type of generative model that learns the underlying distribution of a dataset using the encoder-decoder structure. VAE has a probabilistic perspective on the input data, and it learns to model the conditional probability of the input data given the latent representation. VAEs allow for the generation of new data based on the learned distribution.

The key difference between the two models is that while autoencoders compress the input data to a single point in the latent space, VAEs use the encoder to map the input data to a probability distribution in the latent space. The decoder then generates a point (sample) from this distribution, allowing VAEs to generate new data points that are not necessarily identical to any of the input samples.

Implementing both models in Keras is relatively straightforward. Here's a quick example of how to implement an autoencoder and a VAE using the Keras framework:

Autoencoder implementation:

```
from keras.layers import Input, Dense
from keras.models import Model

# Define input layer
input_layer = Input(shape=(input_dim,))

# Define encoder
encoder_layer = Dense(128, activation='relu')(input_layer)
encoder_layer = Dense(encoding_dim, activation='relu')(encoder_layer)

# Define decoder
decoder_layer = Dense(128, activation='relu')(encoder_layer)
decoder_layer = Dense(input_dim, activation='sigmoid')(decoder_layer)

# Define the entire model
autoencoder = Model(input_layer, decoder_layer)

# Compile the model
autoencoder.compile(optimizer='adam', loss='binary_crossentropy')
```

Variational Autoencoder implementation:

```
from keras.layers import Input, Dense, Lambda
from keras.models import Model
from keras import backend as K
import numpy as np
```

```
# Define input layer
input_layer = Input(shape=(input_dim,))

# Define encoder
encoder_layer = Dense(128, activation='relu')(input_layer)
encoder_layer = Dense(64, activation='relu')(encoder_layer)

# Define mean and standard deviation layers
latent_dim = 2
mean_layer = Dense(latent_dim)(encoder_layer)
log_var_layer = Dense(latent_dim)(encoder_layer)

# Define the sampling function
def sampling(args):
    mean, log_var = args
    epsilon = K.random_normal(shape=K.shape(mean), mean=0., stddev=1.)
    return mean + K.exp(log_var / 2) * epsilon

# Define the latent space sampling layer
latent_layer = Lambda(sampling)([mean_layer, log_var_layer])

# Define decoder
decoder_layer = Dense(64, activation='relu')(latent_layer)
decoder_layer = Dense(128, activation='relu')(decoder_layer)
decoder_layer = Dense(input_dim, activation='sigmoid')(decoder_layer)

# Define the entire model
vae = Model(input_layer, decoder_layer)

# Define the loss function
reconstruction_loss = K.sum(K.binary_crossentropy(input_layer, decoder_layer),
    axis=-1)
kl_loss = -0.5 * K.sum(1 + log_var_layer - K.square(mean_layer) - K.exp(
    log_var_layer), axis=-1)
vae_loss = K.mean(reconstruction_loss + kl_loss)

# Compile the model
vae.add_loss(vae_loss)
vae.compile(optimizer='adam')
```

In summary, while autoencoders are great for data compression and reconstruction, VAEs can learn the underlying distribution of a dataset and generate new data samples. Both of these models are powerful tools in the field of deep learning, and Keras makes it easy to implement them with just a few lines of code!

4.14 How do you perform model ensembling in Keras, and what are the advantages of this approach?

Model ensembling is a technique where multiple models are trained separately and their predictions are combined to produce a final prediction. In Keras, model ensembling can be done in several ways, including:

1. Averaging the predictions of multiple models: This involves training multiple models with different hyperparameters or architectures
and combining their predictions by taking the average. For example,
if three models predict the target variable to be 0.6, 0.7, and 0.8,
respectively, the ensemble prediction would be $(0.6 + 0.7 + 0.8)/3 =$
0.7. This can be easily implemented by using the Keras API to load
and predict each model separately and then taking the average of the
results.

2. Stacking models: In this approach, multiple models are trained
and their predictions are used as inputs to a meta-model that learns
how to combine them to produce a final prediction. The meta-model
can be trained using the predictions of the base models along with
the true labels to learn how to combine the predictions. Again, this
can be done easily in Keras by training the base models separately
and then using their predictions as input to the meta-model.

Advantages of model ensembling:

1. Improved performance: Ensemble models are known to have better
predictive performance than individual models. By combining the
predictions of multiple models, we can reduce overfitting and increase
the stability of the predictions.

2. Robustness: Ensemble models are generally more robust to noise
and outliers in the data. Since the predictions of multiple models are
combined, the effect of errors in one model is minimized.

3. Balanced performance: Ensemble models can help to balance the
performance of different models, by combining models with different
strengths and weaknesses. For example, one model may be good at
predicting one aspect of the data, while another model may be better
at another aspect.

4. Flexibility: Model ensembling can be easily adapted to different
types of models, including neural networks, decision trees, and linear
models.

In summary, model ensembling is a powerful technique for improving
the performance and robustness of machine learning models. Keras
provides easy-to-use tools for implementing ensemble models, making

it a popular choice for building complex models.

4.15 What is the purpose of using Keras with a distributed training framework like Horovod or TensorFlow's tf.distribute?

Keras is a high-level neural network API written in Python for building and training deep learning models. It provides an easy-to-use interface to design complex neural networks and its APIs are designed to be user-friendly and intuitivewhich makes the process of building and training models faster and more efficient.

However, deep learning models can be computationally intensive and require significant computational resources to train on large datasets. To speed up the training process, one can use a distributed training framework like Horovod or TensorFlow's tf.distribute, which enables distributed computing across multiple GPUs or machines.

The purpose of using Keras with a distributed training framework is to achieve faster and more scalable training of deep learning models. By utilizing distributed training, one can parallelize the training process across multiple nodes and GPUs, which can reduce the training time and achieve higher throughput.

One of the most significant advantages of using Keras with a distributed training framework like Horovod or TensorFlow's tf.distribute is that the user can continue to use Keras's high-level APIs while leveraging the full power of distributed training. The user can write Keras code the same way they would for a single GPU/machine, and the distributed training framework will handle the distribution of the workload transparently.

For example, if we have a deep learning model built using Keras that takes a long time to train on a single GPU, we can distribute the training using Horovod or TensorFlow's tf.distribute. This will enable us to train our model on multiple GPUs or machines in parallel, significantly reducing the training time and allowing us to scale up our training to larger, more complex models and datasets.

In summary, using Keras with a distributed training framework like Horovod or TensorFlow's tf.distribute enables faster and more scalable training of deep learning models by parallelizing the training process across multiple GPUs or machines while still allowing the user to leverage the high-level APIs provided by Keras.

4.16   Can you explain the concept of curriculum learning, and how it can be applied in a Keras model?

Curriculum Learning is a training scheme where we train a deep learning model on easy samples first and gradually increase the difficulty level of the training samples. It is an effective way of preventing the model from getting trapped in a suboptimal solution, which can happen if it is trained only on difficult samples. The idea behind curriculum learning is that it mimics how humans learn new concepts; we start with the basics and move on to more complex topics.

Curriculum Learning can be applied in Keras models by progressively increasing the difficulty of the training samples. This can be achieved by sorting the training samples based on their difficulty level using some pre-defined metrics. For example, in the case of object recognition, we can sort the training samples based on their object size. We can start training the model on the small objects first and slowly increase the size of the objects.

In Keras, we can implement curriculum learning by defining a custom data generator for our training data. We can then use this generator to load the training samples in a sorted order based on their difficulty level. We can use the 'sample_weight' parameter in Keras to assign weights to each sample based on its difficulty level. This will ensure that the model pays more attention to the difficult samples during training.

Another approach to implementing curriculum learning in Keras is by using transfer learning. In transfer learning, we initially train the model on a smaller set of easy samples and then fine-tune it on harder samples. This way, the model learns a good initial representation of the problem and then optimizes it for more complex variations.

Overall, curriculum learning can be a powerful tool for training deep learning models, especially in cases where the data instances differ significantly in difficulty level. By starting with easy samples and gradually increasing the difficulty level, we can ensure that the model learns a more robust and representative representation of the problem.

4.17 How do you implement custom training loops in Keras, and when would you need to do so?

In Keras, a custom training loop can be implemented using the 'tf.GradientTape' API. The 'GradientTape' API allows us to trace operations for computing gradients using the 'tf.Variable' API, which enables us to define and update our model's parameters explicitly.

To implement a custom training loop in Keras, we need to do the following:

- 1. Define our model

- 2. Specify the loss function

- 3. Instantiate an optimizer

- 4. Write the training loop using 'tf.GradientTape'

Here's an example of implementing a custom training loop in Keras:

```
import tensorflow as tf

# Define our model
model = tf.keras.Sequential([
    tf.keras.layers.Dense(10, activation='relu', input_shape=(784,)),
    tf.keras.layers.Dense(10)
])

# Specify the loss function
loss_fn = tf.keras.losses.SparseCategoricalCrossentropy(from_logits=True)

# Instantiate an optimizer
optimizer = tf.keras.optimizers.Adam()
```

```
# Load the MNIST dataset
(x_train, y_train), _ = tf.keras.datasets.mnist.load_data()
x_train = x_train.reshape(60000, 784).astype('float32') / 255
y_train = y_train.astype('float32')

# Define the training loop using tf.GradientTape
@tf.function
def train_step(x, y):
    with tf.GradientTape() as tape:
        # Make a prediction on all the batch
        logits = model(x)
        # Compute the loss value for this batch
        loss_value = loss_fn(y, logits)
    # Use the gradient tape to automatically retrieve
    # the gradients of the trainable variables with respect to the loss.
    grads = tape.gradient(loss_value, model.trainable_weights)
    # Run one step of gradient descent by updating
    # the value of the variables to minimize the loss.
    optimizer.apply_gradients(zip(grads, model.trainable_weights))
    return loss_value

# Run the training loop over multiple epochs
for epoch in range(epochs):
    print("Epoch {}/{}".format(epoch + 1, epochs))

    # Shuffle the training data for each epoch
    indices = tf.random.shuffle(tf.range(len(x_train)))
    x_train = tf.gather(x_train, indices)
    y_train = tf.gather(y_train, indices)

    # Divide the training data into batches
    for step in range(len(x_train) // batch_size):
        x_batch = x_train[step * batch_size:(step + 1) * batch_size]
        y_batch = y_train[step * batch_size:(step + 1) * batch_size]

        # Run the custom training loop
        loss_value = train_step(x_batch, y_batch)

    print("Training loss: {}".format(loss_value))
```

Now, let's discuss when we might need to implement a custom training loop in Keras. The most common use case is to implement a model with custom training logic that cannot be expressed in the standard Keras API. For example, we may need to apply a custom algorithm to adjust the learning rate of our optimizer during training or implement our regularization techniques.

Another reason for using a custom training loop is to improve performance by using custom data loading and preprocessing methods. In some cases, the standard Keras API for loading data may not be optimal, and writing a custom data loading pipeline can improve performance significantly.

In summary, implementing custom training loops in Keras is an advanced technique that offers a lot of flexibility and control over the training process. It's typically used when we need to implement custom training logic that cannot be achieved using the standard Keras

API, and it can be an excellent way to improve performance in some situations.

4.18 What are some best practices for managing memory usage and optimizing performance when training large-scale models in Keras?

Training large-scale neural network models in Keras can be computationally expensive and memory intensive. Therefore, managing memory usage and optimizing performance are crucial for successful model training. Here are some best practices for managing memory usage and optimizing performance when training large-scale models in Keras:

1. Batch Size: Batch size is the number of samples that are forwarded through the network during each iteration of the training process. Choosing a larger batch size can help increase training speed, but it can also demand more memory. Therefore, it is important to choose a batch size that can be processed efficiently while not exceeding the memory capacity of the hardware.

2. Early Stopping: One common technique to avoid overfitting is early stopping. This technique monitors the performance of the model on a validation dataset and stops the training process when the performance of the model on the validation dataset stops improving. This has the advantage of reducing training time and improving the generalization ability of the model.

3. Model Architecture: Optimizing neural network architecture can have a significant impact on performance. Using simpler models, reducing the number of layers, and adjusting the number of neurons in each layer is a common way to reduce memory usage while maintaining good performance. Furthermore, using techniques such as transfer learning, model compression, and pruning can help reduce the size of the model while maintaining its accuracy.

4. Regularization: Regularization techniques such as L1/L2 regular-

ization, dropout, and batch normalization can help prevent overfitting and improve the generalization of the model.

5. Hardware Optimization: Choosing the appropriate hardware configuration can also impact training speed and memory usage. Using a machine with more memory, using GPUs, or using distributed training can all help optimize the performance of the model.

6. Data Augmentation: Data augmentation is the technique of generating new training data by applying transformations such as rotations, scaling, and cropping to the original data. This technique can help prevent overfitting of the model by generating additional data for training, thereby reducing the reliance on a limited amount of training data.

7. Memory Management: Finally, there are several techniques to optimize memory usage such as using Keras callbacks to clear memory after each epoch, using generators to generate data in batches, or reducing the amount of monitoring on the training process.

Implementing and optimizing these strategies can help effectively manage memory usage and optimize performance when training large-scale models in Keras.

4.19 How do you use Keras to perform transfer learning across different modalities, such as images and text?

Transfer learning is a powerful technique in deep learning that allows us to leverage pre-trained models and transfer their knowledge to solve new tasks with less data and less training time. Keras provides an easy way to perform transfer learning across different modalities, such as images and text, using its Functional API.

To perform transfer learning across different modalities, we can take the following steps:

1. Load the pre-trained model: First, we need to load a pre-trained model that has been trained on a large dataset. For example, we can

use a pre-trained image classifier such as VGG16 to perform image recognition tasks, or we can use a pre-trained text model like BERT to perform natural language processing tasks.

```
from keras.applications import VGG16, MobileNet
from keras.models import Model

image_model = VGG16(weights='imagenet', include_top=False)
text_model = MobileNet(weights='imagenet', include_top=False)
```

2. Freeze the layers: Next, we need to freeze the layers of the pre-trained models so that the weights are not updated during training. This is important because we want to use the pre-trained weights to extract features and not retrain them on our specific dataset.

```
for layer in image_model.layers:
    layer.trainable = False
for layer in text_model.layers:
    layer.trainable = False
```

3. Define the model architecture: Now we can define the architecture of our transfer learning model, which consists of the pre-trained models and additional layers for the new task. For example, we can concatenate the output features of the image and text models and add a few dense layers for classification.

```
from keras.layers import Input, concatenate, Dense

image_input = Input(shape=(224, 224, 3))
text_input = Input(shape=(max_seq_length,))

image_features = image_model(image_input)
text_features = text_model(text_input)

merged_features = concatenate([image_features, text_features])
dense1 = Dense(256, activation='relu')(merged_features)
dense2 = Dense(128, activation='relu')(dense1)
output = Dense(num_classes, activation='softmax')(dense2)

model = Model(inputs=[image_input, text_input], outputs=output)
```

4. Compile and train the model: Finally, we need to compile and train the transfer learning model. We can use the same optimizers, loss functions, and metrics as we would for any other Keras model.

```
model.compile(optimizer='adam', loss='categorical_crossentropy', metrics=['
    accuracy'])
model.summary()

model.fit([train_images, train_text], train_labels, epochs=10, batch_size=32,
    validation_data=([val_images, val_text], val_labels))
```

By following these steps, we can easily perform transfer learning across different modalities in Keras. This allows us to leverage the pre-trained knowledge from one domain to solve tasks in another domain even with limited data.

4.20   Can you explain the concept of learning rate scheduling in Keras, and how it can be used to improve model convergence?

Learning rate scheduling is a technique used in deep learning algorithms to improve model convergence by gradually decreasing the learning rate over time. The learning rate is a hyperparameter that controls the step size taken by the optimizer during training to update the weights of the neural network. A smaller learning rate means slower convergence, but is less likely to miss the optimal solution, while a larger learning rate speeds up training, but is more likely to result in overshooting the optimal solution.

Learning rate scheduling is motivated by the observation that a large learning rate at the beginning of training can result in large weight updates, which may cause the model to move in the wrong direction and miss the optimal solution. By gradually decreasing the learning rate over time, we can reduce the step size taken by the optimizer, making it easier for the model to converge to the optimal solution.

In Keras, there are several popular learning rate schedules that can be used, including:

1. Step Decay: This schedule drops the learning rate by a factor after a fixed number of training epochs. For example, we can reduce the learning rate by a factor of 0.1 after every 10 epochs, i.e., setting 'decay_rate = learning_rate / 10', where 'learning_rate' is the initial learning rate, and 'decay_rate' is the new learning rate after every step.

2. Exponential Decay: This schedule drops the learning rate exponentially over time. For example, we can set the learning rate as a function of the epoch number, 'learning_rate = learning_rate0 * e(-kt)', where 'learning_rate0' is the initial learning rate, 'k' is the

decay rate, and 't' is the epoch number.

3. Cosine Annealing: This schedule drops the learning rate according to a cosine function over time. The learning rate is given by 'learning_rate = learning_rate0 * 0.5 * (1 + cos(epoch / T))', where 'T' is the number of epochs after which the learning rate restarts.

Applying a learning rate schedule can improve model convergence by reducing the chance of the model overshooting the optimal solution or getting stuck in a local minimum during training. By using a learning rate schedule, the model can still take large steps at the beginning of training when the weights are far from the optimal solution, but gradually decrease the step size as the weights get closer to the optimal solution.

Chapter 5

Expert

5.1 Can you explain the concept of neural architecture search (NAS), and how it can be applied using Keras?

Neural architecture search (NAS) is the process of automating the task of designing architectures for neural networks. The goal of NAS is to find the architecture that performs best for a particular task, such as image classification or natural language processing, without requiring human expertise or trial-and-error experimentation.

There are several approaches to NAS, including evolutionary algorithms, reinforcement learning, and gradient-based methods. In gradient-based methods, the search for a good architecture is viewed as an optimization problem, and the architecture is updated iteratively based on the gradient of the validation error. This requires training and evaluating a large number of architectures, which can be computationally expensive.

Keras provides an easy-to-use framework for implementing NAS using both evolutionary algorithms and reinforcement learning. One way to implement NAS in Keras is to define a search space of possible architectures, which can include different layer types, activation functions,

and hyperparameters such as the number of neurons per layer. One
can then train a population of architectures in parallel, evaluate their
performance on a validation set, and use their performance to guide
the search for better architectures.

For example, here is a basic template for implementing NAS in Keras
using reinforcement learning:

```python
from keras.layers import *
from keras.models import Sequential
from keras.optimizers import *
from keras.callbacks import EarlyStopping
from keras.datasets import mnist
from keras import backend as K
import random

# define search space of possible architectures
layer_types = [Conv2D, Dense, MaxPooling2D, Dropout]
activation_functions = ['relu', 'sigmoid', 'tanh']
num_neurons = [32, 64, 128]

# define reward function (validation accuracy)
def reward_function(model):
    (x_train, y_train), (x_test, y_test) = mnist.load_data()
    model.compile(loss='categorical_crossentropy', optimizer=Adam(lr=0.01),
      metrics=['accuracy'])
    model.fit(x_train, y_train, batch_size=128, epochs=10, validation_data=(
      x_test, y_test), callbacks=[EarlyStopping(patience=3)])
    _, val_acc = model.evaluate(x_test, y_test, verbose=0)
    return val_acc

# define function to generate random architecture
def generate_architecture():
    model = Sequential()
    num_layers = random.choice(range(1, 4))
    for i in range(num_layers):
        layer_type = random.choice(layer_types)
        activation = random.choice(activation_functions)
        neurons = random.choice(num_neurons)
        kwargs = {}
        if layer_type == Conv2D:
            kwargs['filters'] = random.choice([16, 32, 64])
            kwargs['kernel_size'] = random.choice([(3, 3), (5, 5), (7, 7)])
            kwargs['padding'] = 'same'
            kwargs['activation'] = activation
        elif layer_type == Dense:
            kwargs['units'] = neurons
            kwargs['activation'] = activation
        elif layer_type == MaxPooling2D:
            kwargs['pool_size'] = random.choice([(2, 2), (3, 3)])
        elif layer_type == Dropout:
            kwargs['rate'] = random.choice([0.25, 0.5, 0.75])
        layer = layer_type(**kwargs)
        model.add(layer)
    model.add(Flatten())
    model.add(Dense(10, activation='softmax'))
    return model

# define function to update architecture based on reward
def update_architecture(model, reward):
    weights = model.get_weights()
    std = K.std(reward)
    normalized_reward = (reward - K.mean(reward)) / (std + 1e-7)
    for i, layer in enumerate(model.layers):
```

```
    if hasattr(layer, 'kernel'):
        layer_weights = weights[i]
        new_weights = layer_weights + 0.01 * normalized_reward * K.
    random_normal(K.shape(layer_weights), mean=0., stddev=1.)
        layer.kernel = new_weights
# main loop for NAS
population_size = 10
num_generations = 20
population = [generate_architecture() for _ in range(population_size)]
for generation in range(num_generations):
    print("Generation", generation+1)
    rewards = K.stack([reward_function(model) for model in population])
    update_architecture(population, rewards)
    best_model = population[K.argmax(rewards)]
    best_reward = rewards[K.argmax(rewards)]
    print("Best validation accuracy:", float(best_reward))
```

In this example, we define a search space of possible architectures that
includes different types of layers, activation functions, and hyperparameters. We then generate a population of random architectures
and evaluate their performance using a validation set. We use a reinforcement learning approach to update the architecture based on the
validation accuracy, and repeat this process for multiple generations.

Overall, using NAS to automatically search for neural network architectures can greatly reduce the time and expertise required to build
high-performance models, and Keras provides a user-friendly framework for implementing NAS using both evolutionary algorithms and
reinforcement learning.

5.2   How do you implement multi-task learning in Keras, and what are the main challenges involved?

Multi-task learning (MTL) involves training a model to perform multiple related tasks simultaneously. In Keras, we can implement MTL
by creating a model with multiple outputs, where each output corresponds to a different task.

Here's an example of a multi-task model in Keras:

```
input_layer = keras.layers.Input(shape=(input_shape))

# shared layers
shared_layer1 = keras.layers.Dense(64, activation='relu')(input_layer)
shared_layer2 = keras.layers.Dense(32, activation='relu')(shared_layer1)
```

```
# task-specific layers
output1 = keras.layers.Dense(10, activation='softmax', name='output1')(
    shared_layer2)
output2 = keras.layers.Dense(1, activation='sigmoid', name='output2')(
    shared_layer2)

model = keras.models.Model(inputs=input_layer, outputs=[output1, output2])
```

In this example, there are two tasks: a multi-class classification task (output1) and a binary classification task (output2). The model has a shared layer (shared_layer2) that is used by both tasks to extract features from the input data, followed by task-specific layers (output1 and output2) that produce the output for each task.

When training the model, we need to provide multiple sets of labels (one for each task) and specify a loss function for each output. For example, we can use categorical cross-entropy for the multi-class task and binary cross-entropy for the binary task:

```
model.compile(optimizer='adam',
              loss={'output1': 'categorical_crossentropy', 'output2': '
    binary_crossentropy'})
```

During training, the model will optimize both losses simultaneously, using backpropagation to update the shared layer and task-specific layers.

One challenge with multi-task learning is balancing the contribution of each task to the overall loss function. If one task is much easier than the others, it may have a disproportionate impact on the model's training. One way to address this is to use a weighted loss function that gives more weight to the harder task.

Another challenge is determining the optimal shared layer architecture to use. The shared layer needs to be expressive enough to capture relevant features for all tasks, but not so complex that it overfits to one or more tasks. Regularization techniques (such as dropout and weight decay) can help prevent overfitting.

5.3   What is the purpose of using a Bayesian optimization approach for hyperparameter tuning in Keras, and how can you implement it?

Hyperparameter tuning is the process of finding the set of hyperparameters that results in the best performance of a deep learning model. These hyperparameters can be anything from the learning rate, the number of layers, the number of neurons in each layer, etc. Finding the best set of hyperparameters is often a difficult task, as there are many possible combinations to try, and it can be time-consuming and computationally expensive to evaluate each one of them.

Bayesian optimization is an approach to hyperparameter tuning that tries to find the best set of hyperparameters by building a probabilistic model of the objective function that we want to optimize. This model represents our belief about the objective function, based on the observations we have made so far. By using this model, we can select, for each iteration, the hyperparameters that are most likely to improve the objective function, taking into account the uncertainties in our model.

The main advantage of using Bayesian optimization is that it can be more efficient than other methods, as it can identify promising hyperparameters more quickly and avoid exploring unpromising ones. It can also handle noisy and non-convex objective functions, which are common in deep learning.

To implement Bayesian optimization in Keras, we can use a library such as Keras Tuner or Hyperopt. Keras Tuner provides a simple and easy-to-use API for hyperparameter tuning, including Bayesian optimization. Here's an example of how to use Keras Tuner to perform Bayesian optimization for a simple Keras model:

```
from tensorflow import keras
from tensorflow.keras import layers
from kerastuner.tuners import BayesianOptimization

def build_model(hp):
    model = keras.Sequential()
    model.add(layers.Dense(units=hp.Int('units', min_value=32, max_value=512,
      step=32),
```

```
                          activation='relu',
                          input_shape=(784,)))
    model.add(layers.Dense(10, activation='softmax'))
    model.compile(optimizer=keras.optimizers.Adam(hp.Choice('learning_rate',
      values=[1e-2, 1e-3, 1e-4])),
                      loss='categorical_crossentropy',
                      metrics=['accuracy'])
    return model

tuner = BayesianOptimization(build_model,
                             objective='val_accuracy',
                             max_trials=10,
                             num_initial_points=3)

tuner.search(x_train, y_train,
             epochs=5,
             validation_data=(x_test, y_test))

best_model = tuner.get_best_models(num_models=1)[0]
```

In this example, we define a search space for the hyperparameters
(in this case, the number of units in the first layer and the learning
rate), and we use Bayesian optimization to find the set of hyperparameters that maximizes the validation accuracy of the model. We
set a maximum number of trials (10) and a number of initial points
to explore (3). We then call the 'search()' method with the training
and validation data, and the tuner performs the optimization process. Finally, we retrieve the best model found by the tuner with the
'get_best_models()' method.

5.4   Can you explain the concept of knowl-edge distillation, and how it can be used in Keras to create smaller, more efficient models?

Knowledge distillation is a technique where a smaller and more efficient model, known as the "student", is trained to mimic the predictions of a larger and more complex model, known as the "teacher".
This is done by training the student on the same dataset as the teacher
model, but instead of predicting the correct output directly, the student tries to match the probability distribution of the teacher's output.

The idea behind knowledge distillation is that the larger teacher model contains a lot of knowledge that may not be necessary to make accurate predictions on a given task. By distilling this knowledge into a smaller student model, we can create an equally accurate model that requires less computational resources and is more efficient to deploy.

In Keras, knowledge distillation can be implemented by creating a new model that takes the input data and trains it to match both the teacher's output and the true output. The loss function used in this new model is a combination of the standard loss function used to train the teacher and a new "distillation loss" that measures the difference between the student's predicted probabilities and the teacher's predicted probabilities. During training, the weights of the teacher model are frozen, and the gradients from the distillation loss are used to update the weights of the student model.

Here's an example of how a knowledge distillation pipeline could be implemented in Keras:

```
# Load the pre-trained teacher model
teacher = load_model('teacher_model.h5')

# Create the student model with smaller architecture
student = create_student_model()

# Define the distillation loss function
def distillation_loss(y_true, y_pred, teacher_pred, temperature):
    # Calculate the soft targets using the teacher's output
    soft_targets = K.softmax(teacher_pred / temperature, axis=-1)
    # Calculate the cross entropy between the soft targets and the student's
      output
    distillation_loss = -K.mean(K.sum(soft_targets * K.log(y_pred), axis=1))
    return distillation_loss

# Define the combined loss function for the student model
def combined_loss(teacher_pred, temperature):
    def loss(y_true, y_pred):
        # Standard categorical cross entropy loss
        ce_loss = K.categorical_crossentropy(y_true, y_pred)
        # Distillation loss
        dist_loss = distillation_loss(y_true, y_pred, teacher_pred, temperature)
        # Final loss as a combination of the two losses
        final_loss = ce_loss + dist_loss
        return final_loss
    return loss

# Freeze the weights of the teacher model
for layer in teacher.layers:
    layer.trainable = False

# Set the temperature for knowledge distillation
temperature = 10

# Create a new model that combines the teacher and student models
input_shape = (None, None, 3)
input_layer = Input(shape=input_shape)
teacher_output = teacher(input_layer)
student_output = student(input_layer)
distilled_loss = combined_loss(teacher_output, temperature)
combined_model = Model(inputs=input_layer, outputs=[teacher_output,
```

```
    student_output]])
combined_model.compile(optimizer='adam', loss=[distilled_loss, '
    categorical_crossentropy'])
```

In this example, the teacher model has already been trained and saved
to disk. We then define the student model with a smaller architecture, and the distillation loss function for measuring the difference
between the soft targets from the teacher model and the student's
predictions. We also define a combined loss function that includes
both the standard categorical cross entropy loss and the distillation
loss.

Next, we freeze the weights of the teacher model so that they are not
updated during training, and create a new model that combines the
input layer and the output layers from both the teacher and student
models. We compile this model with the combined loss function and
train it on the same dataset as the teacher model.

By using knowledge distillation, we can create a more efficient model
that is capable of making accurate predictions on the same task as
the larger teacher model. This technique can be particularly useful
in scenarios where computational resources are limited, such as on
mobile devices or embedded systems.

5.5   How do you implement unsupervised and self-supervised learning techniques using Keras, and what are their main advantages?

Unsupervised and self-supervised learning are two important techniques in deep learning that are used to learn from unlabeled data.
While supervised learning involves training a model using labeled
data, unsupervised learning refers to training models using unlabeled
data.

In Keras, there are several ways to implement unsupervised and self-
supervised learning techniques. Some popular ones are:

1. Autoencoders: Autoencoders are neural networks that are trained

to reconstruct their input. They consist of an encoder that maps the input to a lower-dimensional representation, and a decoder that maps the representation back to the input space. By training the network to minimize the difference between the input and output, the model learns to extract useful features from the data.

For example, let's consider an image autoencoder that takes as input a grayscale image of size 28x28 pixels. The encoder will map this input to a lower-dimensional representation, say 128-dimensional. The decoder will then map this representation back to the original image. By minimizing the reconstruction error, the model learns to encode the most important features of the input image into the 128-dimensional representation.

2. Generative Adversarial Networks (GANs): GANs consist of two neural networks - a generator and a discriminator. The generator takes as input a random noise vector and generates a fake image. The discriminator takes as input a real or fake image and predicts whether it is real or fake. The two networks are trained together, with the generator trying to generate more realistic images, and the discriminator trying to correctly classify them.

For example, let's consider a GAN that is trained to generate images of faces. The generator network takes as input a random noise vector and outputs a 64x64 pixel image. The discriminator network takes as input a 64x64 pixel image and outputs a scalar value indicating whether it is real or fake. By training the two networks together, the generator learns to generate more realistic images of faces, while the discriminator learns to distinguish between real and fake images.

3. Contrastive Predictive Coding (CPC): CPC is a self-supervised learning technique that is often used in natural language processing. The idea behind CPC is to predict the context of a sequence of input data. For example, given a sequence of words in a sentence, the model might be trained to predict the next word in the sequence.

For example, let's consider a CPC model that is trained to predict the next word in a sequence of 10 words. The input to the model might be a vector representation of each word in the sequence, and the output might be a probability distribution over the vocabulary of possible next words. By training the model to maximize the likelihood of predicting the correct next word, the model learns to encode useful information about the context of the input sequence.

The main advantages of unsupervised and self-supervised learning techniques are:

1. They allow us to learn from unlabeled data, which is often easier to come by than labeled data.

2. They can be used to pretrain a model on a large dataset before finetuning on a smaller labeled dataset, which can improve performance.

3. They can be used to learn more abstract and higher-level features of the data, which can be useful for downstream tasks.

In summary, unsupervised and self-supervised learning techniques are important techniques in deep learning that allow us to learn from unlabeled data. Keras provides several ways to implement these techniques, including autoencoders, GANs, and CPC. The main advantages of unsupervised and self-supervised learning include the ability to learn from unlabeled data, pretraining capabilities, and learning useful features of the data.

5.6   What are some advanced techniques for visualizing the learned features and decision-making processes of a Keras model?

There are various advanced techniques for visualizing the learned features and decision-making processes of a Keras model, some of which are:

1. Activation Maximization: This technique involves maximizing the activations of specific neurons in a model by modifying the input to the model. This results in generating an image or pattern that maximally activates the specified neuron. In this way, it is possible to understand what a particular neuron has learned to detect.

2. Grad-CAM: Grad-CAM stands for Gradient-weighted Class Ac-

tivation Mapping. It is a technique that highlights the regions of an image that are most relevant to a particular class output by the model. Essentially, it computes the gradient of the class output with respect to the feature maps and then weights the feature maps according to the gradient values. This technique provides an intuitive understanding of what parts of an image the model attends to while making predictions.

3. t-SNE Visualization: t-SNE (t-distributed stochastic neighbor embedding) is a technique for visualizing high-dimensional data in low-dimensional space. By reducing the dimensionality of the learned features in a Keras model and projecting them in 2D or 3D space, it is possible to visualize the features learned by a model in a way that can be easily interpreted by humans.

4. Integrated Gradients: Integrated Gradients is a technique that provides a way to attribute the contribution of each feature or pixel in an input image to the final prediction of a model. This is achieved by taking the gradient of the output with respect to the input and then integrating this gradient over a path from a baseline input image to the actual input image. This technique helps to understand how the model makes decisions based on specific features of an input image.

5. Filter Visualization: Filter visualization involves generating or synthesizing an input image that maximizes the activation of a particular filter in a convolutional neural network. This provides an understanding of what a particular filter has learned to detect.

There are many more advanced techniques for visualizing the learned features and decision-making processes of a Keras model, these are just a few examples. Each technique has its strengths and weaknesses, and the choice of technique will depend on the specific problem being studied and the goals of the analysis.

5.7   How do you handle out-of-vocabulary (OOV) tokens when working with text data in Keras, and what are some best practices for doing so?

Out-of-vocabulary (OOV) tokens are the words that are not present in the vocabulary or the set of words known to a language model. Handling OOV is crucial in natural language processing (NLP) applications because OOV tokens can negatively affect the performance of a language model.

Here are some ways you can handle OOV tokens in Keras when working with text data:

1. Padding and Truncating: These two techniques are common ways to handle OOV tokens for sentences of different lengths. Padding involves adding zeros or a special token at the end of the sentence to make it the same length as the longest sentence in the dataset. Truncating involves cutting off any words after a specified length. In Keras, you can use 'pad_sequence' to pad or truncate sentences.

```
from keras.preprocessing.sequence import pad_sequences

# Padding
padded_data = pad_sequences(data, maxlen=max_seq_length, padding='post',
    truncating='post')

# Truncating
truncated_data = pad_sequences(data, maxlen=max_seq_length, padding='post',
    truncating='post')
```

2. Using OOV tokens: You can replace OOV tokens with a special token such as '___UNK___' or '<UNK>' to indicate that the word is unknown. During training, the model will learn to treat '___UNK___' as a regular word, and during inference, you can replace any new unknown words with '___UNK___'.

```
from keras.preprocessing.text import Tokenizer

tokenizer = Tokenizer(num_words=vocab_size, oov_token='__UNK__')
tokenizer.fit_on_texts(texts)

# Convert text to sequences
sequences = tokenizer.texts_to_sequences(texts)

# Create the padded sequences
padded_sequences = pad_sequences(sequences, maxlen=max_length, padding='post',
    truncating='post')
```

3. Word Embeddings: Using pre-trained word embeddings such as
GloVe or Word2Vec can help capture the semantic meaning of OOV
tokens. These embeddings are trained on a large corpus of words and
can capture the relationships and similarities between words. During
training, the model can use the pre-trained embeddings to handle
OOV tokens.

```
from keras.layers import Embedding

embedding_matrix = np.zeros((vocab_size, embedding_dim))

for word, i in tokenizer.word_index.items():
    embedding_vector = embeddings_index.get(word)
    if embedding_vector is not None:
        # Words not found in embedding index will be all zeros
        embedding_matrix[i] = embedding_vector

embedding_layer = Embedding(vocab_size,
                            embedding_dim,
                            weights=[embedding_matrix],
                            trainable=False)

# Define the model
model = Sequential()
model.add(embedding_layer)
```

Best practices for handling OOV tokens in Keras are:

```
1. Preprocessing text data to remove irrelevant words and normalize the text.
2. Use a large vocabulary size to reduce the probability of OOV tokens.
3. Use pre-trained embeddings where possible to handle OOV tokens.
4. Use padding and truncating to handle sentences of varying lengths.
5. Evaluate the performance of the model on test data to ensure that the model
     is not biased towards OOV tokens.
```

Overall, handling OOV tokens is crucial in NLP applications, and
using the techniques mentioned above can help improve the performance of your language model.

5.8 Can you explain the concept of continual learning, and how it can be implemented in Keras to allow models to adapt to new data over time?

Continual learning, sometimes referred to as lifelong learning, is the
process of incrementally updating a machine learning model over
time, as new data becomes available. This is in contrast to traditional machine learning, where a model is often trained once on a

fixed dataset, and then used to make predictions on new data.

Continual learning is particularly relevant in scenarios where new data is constantly being generated, and the model needs to be updated to reflect changes in its environment. For example, in a recommendation system for an e-commerce platform, the model might need to be updated as new products are added to the catalog, or as user preferences change.

To implement continual learning in Keras, there are a few key techniques that can be used. One common strategy is to use incremental model learning, where the model is trained on new data in a sequential manner, rather than retraining the entire model from scratch. This can be done by freezing the weights of the existing layers in the model, and only training the newly added layers on the new data. This approach can help to alleviate the problem of catastrophic forgetting, where the model forgets what it has previously learned when new data is introduced.

Another approach is to use regularization techniques, such as weight decay or dropout, to help prevent overfitting of the model to the new data. This can help to ensure that the model continues to generalize well to new data, even as it is updated over time.

Finally, it is important to monitor the performance of the model over time, and to adjust the learning rate or other hyperparameters as needed to ensure that the model continues to learn and adapt effectively.

Overall, continual learning is an important technique for enabling machine learning models to adapt to changing environments over time, and can be implemented effectively in Keras using a variety of techniques.

5.9   What are the main challenges of scaling Keras models to work with large datasets, and what are some techniques to overcome these challenges?

The main challenges of scaling Keras models to work with large datasets are memory constraints, computation time, and overfitting.

Memory constraints arise when loading large datasets into memory, especially when working with high-resolution images or text data. This can quickly exhaust the available GPU memory, leading to crashes or suboptimal performance.

Computation time is another major challenge, as training large models with many layers and parameters can take days or even weeks. This is especially challenging when fine-tuning pre-trained models, where the initial layers may be fixed and only the final layers are trained to adapt to the new dataset.

Overfitting is a third challenge when scaling Keras models to larger datasets. With more data, it becomes easier for the model to memorize the training data rather than learn generalizable patterns.

To overcome these challenges, there are several techniques you can use:

1. Data generators and batch processing: Rather than loading the entire dataset into memory, generators allow you to stream the data in batches, reducing memory usage and avoiding crashes. This approach also allows for data augmentation techniques to be applied on-the-fly, further improving model performance.

2. Model parallelism: For extremely large models with many layers, distributing the computation across multiple GPUs or CPUs can reduce training time and memory constraints.

3. Regularization techniques: To mitigate overfitting, regularization techniques such as dropout, L1/L2 weight decay, and early stopping can be applied.

4. Transfer Learning: Fine-tuning a pre-trained model can signifi-

cantly reduce computation time and memory constraints, while still achieving state-of-the-art performance on a new dataset.

5. Gradient Accumulation and Mixed Precision Training: Gradient accumulation which accumulate gradients over multiple batches and update weights once in a specified period of time can help reduce the memory utilized in training. Mixed precision training which involves using half-precision floating point for the activations and gradients in the forward-, and back-propagation steps can reduce the memory requirement while maintaining the similar training time.

Overall, by applying these techniques, it is possible to scale Keras models to work with large datasets, and achieve state-of-the-art performance on a range of tasks.

5.10   How do you use Keras to perform multi-modal learning, where the model must process and integrate data from multiple sources or modalities?

Multi-modal learning involves processing and integrating information from multiple sources or modalities, such as images, audio, text, and numerical data. Keras provides several ways to perform multi-modal learning, and I will describe two common approaches in detail:

1. Model Fusion: With model fusion, we create separate models to process data from each modality, and then combine them into one unified model that processes and integrates all the modalities. The output of each modal model is concatenated, and this concatenated output is fed into a fully connected layer or an LSTM layer for the final classification. Here is an example code snippet for multi-modal learning using model fusion in Keras:

```
from keras.models import Model, Sequential
from keras.layers import Input, Dense, LSTM, concatenate

# define input layers for each modality
input_audio = Input(shape=(audio_features,))
input_image = Input(shape=(image_size, image_size, num_channels))

# define models for each modality
audio_model = Sequential()
```

```
audio_model.add(LSTM(64, return_sequences=False, input_shape=(max_audio_len,
    audio_features)))
audio_model.add(Dense(32, activation='relu'))

image_model = Sequential()
image_model.add(Conv2D(32, kernel_size=(3, 3), activation='relu', input_shape=(
    image_size, image_size, num_channels)))
image_model.add(MaxPooling2D(pool_size=(2, 2)))
image_model.add(Flatten())

# concatenate outputs from both modal models
merged = concatenate([audio_model.output, image_model.output])

# add a fully connected layer for classification
merged = Dense(64, activation='relu')(merged)
merged = Dense(num_classes, activation='softmax')(merged)

# create the final model
multi_modal_model = Model(inputs=[audio_model.input, image_model.input], outputs
    =merged)
multi_modal_model.compile(loss='categorical_crossentropy', optimizer='adam')
```

2. Shared Layers: With shared layers, we create a single neural network with shared layers that can learn to extract features from each modality. In this approach, each modality is processed by a set of shared layers, and the outputs from each set of shared layers are concatenated and fed into a set of fully connected layers for classification. This approach can be computationally efficient as we do not need to train multiple independent models for each modality. Here is an example code snippet for multi-modal learning using shared layers in Keras:

```
from keras.layers import Conv2D, MaxPooling2D, Flatten, Dense, LSTM
from keras.models import Model
from keras.layers import Input
from keras.layers.merge import concatenate

# define the input layers for each modality
input_audio = Input(shape=(max_audio_len, audio_features))
input_image = Input(shape=(image_size, image_size, num_channels))

# define the shared layers
shared_cnn = Sequential()
shared_cnn.add(Conv2D(32, kernel_size=(3, 3), activation='relu', input_shape=(
    image_size, image_size, num_channels)))
shared_cnn.add(MaxPooling2D(pool_size=(2, 2)))
shared_cnn.add(Flatten())

shared_rnn = Sequential()
shared_rnn.add(LSTM(64, return_sequences=False))
shared_rnn.add(Dense(32, activation='relu'))

# process each modality using the shared layers
processed_audio = shared_rnn(input_audio)
processed_image = shared_cnn(input_image)

# concatenate the output from each modality processor
merged = concatenate([processed_audio, processed_image])

# add additional fully connected layers for classification
merged = Dense(64, activation='relu')(merged)
merged = Dense(num_classes, activation='softmax')(merged)
```

```
# create the final model
multi_modal_model = Model(inputs=[input_audio, input_image], outputs=merged)
multi_modal_model.compile(loss='categorical_crossentropy', optimizer='adam')
```

In summary, multi-modal learning with Keras can be implemented using either model fusion or shared layers. Through these approaches, Keras provides the flexibility to process and integrate multiple types of data and develop complex deep learning models that can improve the performance of many applications.

5.11   Can you explain the concept of meta-learning, and how it can be applied using Keras to learn new tasks more quickly?

Meta-learning, also known as "learning to learn," is a subfield of machine learning that focuses on developing algorithms that can quickly learn new tasks from a small number of examples. In other words, meta-learning models are designed to generalize from past experiences and apply that knowledge to new tasks in a more efficient manner.

Meta-learning can be applied to a wide range of tasks, including image classification, natural language processing, and robotics. One common approach to meta-learning is to use a meta-learner model that is trained on a diverse set of tasks, and then used to learn new tasks with minimal data.

In the context of Keras, meta-learning can be implemented using techniques such as transfer learning and few-shot learning. Transfer learning involves using a pre-trained neural network as a starting point for a new task, and fine-tuning the parameters to optimize performance on the specific task.

Few-shot learning, on the other hand, involves training a model on a small number of examples per class, and then testing its ability to generalize to new examples. This approach can be applied in a meta-learning context by using a small number of examples from multiple tasks to train a meta-learner model, which can then be used to quickly adapt to new tasks.

To illustrate this concept with an example, imagine you are training a model to recognize different types of animals. Instead of training a new model from scratch each time you encounter a new animal, you could use a meta-learner model that has been trained on a wide range of animal classifications. Then, when you encounter a new animal, you could use the meta-learner model to quickly learn features that distinguish that animal from others, and fine-tune the model for optimal performance.

Overall, meta-learning is an exciting area of research that holds promise for enabling more efficient and flexible machine learning systems. By leveraging past experiences to quickly adapt to new situations, meta-learning models could enable a wide range of applications in domains such as robotics, natural language processing, and more.

5.12   What are some techniques for improving the interpretability and explainability of deep learning models in Keras?

Interpretability and explainability are essential for building trust and confidence in deep learning models. Here are some techniques that can help to improve the interpretability and explainability of deep learning models in Keras:

1. Visualization of model architecture and training progress: Visualization is an effective way of explaining how a deep learning model is working. Keras provides a range of tools to visualize the model architecture like 'model.summary()' and 'plot_model()' methods. Additionally, by plotting the training and validation loss and accuracy curves, one can understand more about model performance and behavior over time.

2. Layer activations and feature visualization: It is crucial to know which part of the input is important to the models prediction. In Keras, one can visualize the input-output relationship by examining

the feature maps created by the layers. This can be helpful in understanding the internal representations of the model.

3. Gradient-weighted Class Activation Mapping (Grad-CAM): Grad-CAM is a technique that highlights which part of an input image the model is paying attention to while making a prediction. This technique can be applied to any convolutional neural network (CNN) model, and Keras provides a convenient way to implement it.

4. LIME and SHAP: LIME (Local Interpretable Model-Agnostic Explanations) and SHAP (SHapley Additive exPlanations) are model-agnostic techniques for explaining the output of any machine learning model. The basic idea behind both is to perturb the input data and observe how the model's output changes. Keras provides support for LIME through its lime package, and the SHAP package can be used with any model.

5. Attention Mechanisms: Attention mechanisms can create heatmaps that highlight important parts of the input that the model is using to make predictions. Attention mechanisms have been used in image captioning, machine translation, and other NLP tasks. Keras offers a range of attention mechanisms that can be used with RNN models.

In summary, there are various techniques and approaches that can be used to improve the interpretability and explainability of deep learning models in Keras. These methods are essential for gaining a better understanding of how the models function and making informed decisions when making predictions based on the models.

5.13 How do you use Keras to perform zero-shot or few-shot learning, where models must generalize to new classes without seeing any labeled examples?

Zero-shot and few-shot learning have become attractive alternatives to traditional supervised learning methods, as they allow us to build models that can generalize to new classes without explicit training on them. These methods are particularly useful in scenarios where it is expensive or time-consuming to obtain labeled data for all possible target classes.

Keras provides multiple tools and methods to perform zero-shot or few-shot learning, such as transfer learning, meta-learning, and reinforcement learning. Here are some of the most commonly used techniques:

1. Transfer Learning: Transfer learning is a technique where pretrained models are used as a starting point for new tasks. The idea is to use the learned features from a pre-trained model on a large dataset (such as ImageNet) and fine-tune them on a smaller dataset with few labeled examples. In Keras, you can perform transfer learning by using pre-trained models such as VGG16, ResNet, or MobileNet, or you can even create your own custom models and fine-tune them for your specific task.

2. Meta-learning: Meta-learning is a technique where models are trained to learn how to learn. In other words, they are trained on a set of tasks to learn a general strategy that can be applied to new tasks. Meta-learning can be performed using various algorithms, such as Model-Agnostic Meta-Learning (MAML), which learns a weight initialization scheme for a given set of tasks, or Prototypical Networks, which learns a metric space where new samples can be classified based on their similarity to a set of prototypes. Keras provides libraries such as TensorFlow Federated and TensorFlow Model Optimization to implement meta-learning models.

3. Reinforcement Learning: Reinforcement learning is a technique where models learn by trial and error through interaction with an environment. This technique can be used for few-shot learning by training models to predict the output of new classes by sampling from an environment in a way similar to the desired task. For instance, you can use RL to train chatbots to answer questions with few labeled examples to start.

In summary, Keras allows you to leverage various techniques to perform zero-shot or few-shot learning, such as transfer learning, meta-learning, and reinforcement learning. With Keras, you can build models that can generalize to new classes without explicit training on them, making it a valuable tool for building powerful machine learning models in challenging scenarios.

5.14   Can you explain the concept of graph neural networks (GNNs) and how they can be implemented using Keras?

Graph neural networks (GNNs) are a type of neural network that can be applied to graph data structures. Graphs can represent a wide range of data, including social networks, biological molecules, transportation networks, and more.

In GNNs, each node in the graph represents an entity in the data, and each edge represents a relationship or connection between entities. The goal of a GNN is to learn a representation of the graph that captures useful information about these relationships and entity attributes.

GNNs typically work by propagating information between neighboring nodes in the graph. This is done through successive iterations of message passing, where each node learns from its neighbors and updates its own representation accordingly. The final representation of each node can then be used for downstream tasks, such as node classification or link prediction.

To implement GNNs in Keras, there are several packages available that provide GNN layers, including GraphSAGE, GAT, GCN, and more. These packages typically include layers that implement message passing for graph data, such as the GraphSAGE layer in the 'stellargraph' package.

Here's an example of a simple GNN architecture implemented with Keras and the 'stellargraph' package:

```
import stellargraph as sg
from stellargraph.layer import GraphSAGE

# define the graph data
G = sg.StellarGraph(nodes=nodes, edges=edges)

# create a GNN model
model = GraphSAGE(layer_sizes=[16, 16], generator=G, bias=True, dropout=0.5)

# compile the model
model.compile(optimizer="adam", loss="categorical_crossentropy")

# train the model
history = model.fit(generator.flow(node_subjects, node_targets), epochs=50)
```

In this example, we define a graph 'G' using the 'stellargraph' package and create a 'GraphSAGE' model with two layers of 16 nodes each, a dropout rate of 0.5, and binary cross-entropy as the loss function. We then compile the model and train it on a set of node subjects and targets using a generator.

5.15   How do you design and implement custom activation functions, and what are some considerations when doing so in Keras?

Keras offers a range of activation functions that can be used in neural networks, but sometimes you may need to design and implement a custom activation function that is specific to your problem domain. Here's how to do it:

To define a custom activation function in Keras, you should define a new class that inherits from Keras' Activation class. The class must implement two methods: ___init___ and ___call___. The ___init___ method is used to initialize the activation function, while the ___call___ method is the one that applies the activation function to the input tensor.

Here's an example of a custom activation function that applies the exponential function to the input:

```
from tensorflow.keras.layers import Activation
from tensorflow.keras import backend as K

class ExpActivation(Activation):
    def __init__(self, activation, **kwargs):
        super(ExpActivation, self).__init__(activation, **kwargs)
        self.__name__ = 'exp_activation'

    def call(self, inputs):
        return K.exp(inputs)
```

Once you've defined your custom activation function, you can use it in your Keras model just like any other activation function. For example:

```
from tensorflow.keras.models import Sequential
from tensorflow.keras.layers import Dense

model = Sequential()
model.add(Dense(64, input_shape=input_shape))
```

```
model.add(ExpActivation('exp'))
```

However, before creating a custom activation function, some considerations should be made:

1. **Differentiability**: Most modern deep learning frameworks like Keras make use of automatic differentiation to compute gradients, which is an important aspect of backpropagation. Being able to compute gradients for activation functions is important for optimizers like stochastic gradient descent (SGD) to be able to update network weights effectively. So, it's crucial that your custom activation function is differentiable.

2. **Monotonicity**: Monotonicity is a mathematical property that says if the input to the function increases, then the output also increases. For example, the ReLU activation function is monotonic since it returns 0 for all negative inputs and linearly increases for all non-negative inputs. Having a monotonic activation function can help speed up convergence during training.

3. **Range of output**: Activation functions output values should be within a certain range. Commonly used ranges are [-1, 1] and [0, 1]. If an activation function's output values are not within the expected range, the training process may break down.

4. **Computational complexity**: Custom activation functions should be computationally efficient. Highly complex activation functions may increase the processing time per sample, slowing down the training process and making it difficult to scale up to larger datasets.

These considerations are important to keep in mind when designing and implementing custom activation functions to ensure that the resulting network trains efficiently, generalizes well to new data and can be optimized effectively.

5.16 What are some techniques for optimizing the deployment of Keras models on edge devices or mobile platforms?

Deploying Keras models on edge devices or mobile platforms requires optimizing both the model architecture and the task of inference. Here are some of the techniques for optimizing the deployment of Keras models on edge devices or mobile platforms-

1. Quantization: Quantization is the process of converting the model weights and activations from float32 to int8 values, which reduces the model size and speeds up computation. The smaller model size in turn reduces the memory requirements for deployment on edge devices. There are several types of quantization, such as dynamic range quantization (DRQ), post-training quantization, and quantization-aware training (QAT). The kind of quantization depends on the model and hardware configuration.

2. Pruning: Pruning a model involves removing unnecessary weights, inputs, or layers. This can reduce the size of the model, as well as speed up inference time by reducing unnecessary computations. Some researchers have proposed using a combination of pruning and quantization to reduce the size of the model even more.

3. Model architecture optimization: When deploying Keras models on edge devices or mobile platforms, it's essential to optimize the model architecture for the device's hardware. For example, mobile GPUs may have a limit on the number of operations they can perform, so models should be designed with smaller layer sizes and fewer layers. Similarly, models with 1x1 convolutional layers rather than dense layers can be more hardware-friendly.

4. On-device inference: Moving inference computations to the edge device instead of sending data to the server can reduce bandwidth and make inference faster. In some cases, this may require porting portions of the model's architecture to the device's hardware or using specialized hardware like TPUs to speed up computation.

5. Knowledge distillation: Knowledge distillation involves training a

smaller "student" model to mimic the behavior of a larger "teacher" model. This technique can be useful when deploying Keras models on edge devices as the smaller model has fewer parameters and can run faster on hardware with limited resources.

In conclusion, optimizing the deployment of Keras models on edge devices or mobile platforms requires a combination of techniques ranging from model architecture optimization to hardware-aware post-training quantization, and from on-device inference to knowledge distillation. By combining the right techniques, developers can create efficient and fast models that deliver excellent results on edge devices and mobile platforms.

5.17   How do you implement active learning in Keras to effectively select samples for labeling and improve model performance with less labeled data?

Active learning is a semi-supervised learning technique that can be used to improve model performance with less labeled data. In active learning, the model selects the most informative data points from the unlabeled dataset and asks the human expert to label them for future use.

Here are the steps to implement active learning in Keras:

1. Train your model on a small labeled data set. This data set should be diverse and representative of the larger population of data you are working with.

2. Use the trained model to make predictions on a set of unlabeled data.

3. Select a subset of the unlabeled data which the model is most uncertain about. These samples are the ones where the model outputs a probability value close to 0.5.

4. Ask the human expert to label the selected subset from step 3.

5. Add the newly labeled data to the labeled data set, retrain the model, and repeat the process of selecting the subset of samples to be labeled until the desired model performance is achieved.

To illustrate how to implement Active Learning in Keras, consider the following example of a binary sentiment classification task:

```
# Step 1: Train the model on a small labeled dataset.
X_train, y_train, X_test, y_test = load_binary_sentiment_data(...)
model = create_binary_sentiment_model(...)
model.fit(X_train, y_train, epochs=10, batch_size=32)

# Step 2: Use the trained model to make predictions on unlabeled data.
X_unlabeled = load_unlabeled_data(...)
predictions = model.predict(X_unlabeled)

# Step 3: Select the most uncertain samples based on the model predictions.
uncertainty_scores = np.abs(predictions - 0.5)
most_uncertain_indices = np.argsort(uncertainty_scores)[:100]

# Step 4: Ask the human expert to label the selected subset.
labeled_data = []
for i in most_uncertain_indices:
  sample = X_unlabeled[i]
  label = expert_label_chooser(sample)
  labeled_data.append((sample, label))

# Step 5: Retrain the model with the newly labeled data and repeat the process.
labeled_samples, labels = zip(*labeled_data)
X_train_new = np.concatenate((X_train, labeled_samples))
y_train_new = np.concatenate((y_train, labels))
model.fit(X_train_new, y_train_new, epochs=10, batch_size=32)
```

In conclusion, Active Learning can be an effective way to select samples for labeling from a large dataset and improve model performance with less labeled data in Keras. It can save time and cost by reducing the labeling process and increasing the efficiency of the model training process.

5.18   Can you explain the concept of capsule networks, and how they can be implemented in Keras to improve model robustness and generalization?

Capsule Networks, also known as CapsNets, are a relatively new neural network architecture that aims to address the limitations of traditional Convolutional Neural Networks (CNNs) in terms of their ability to handle variations in scale, orientation, and deformation. They were introduced by Sara Sabour, Geoffrey E. Hinton, and Nicholas Frosst from the Google Brain Team in their paper titled "Dynamic Routing Between Capsules," which was released in 2017.

The basic idea behind CapsNets is to group neurons, called capsules, that are concerned with modeling the instantiation parameters of a specific type of feature. For example, the capsule may represent the parameters of a line, such as its coordinate in 3D space and its orientation. Each capsule takes as input the output of a lower layer of capsules or convolutional filters, and outputs a prediction of the instantiation parameters, along with a probabilistic value representing the likelihood of the feature existing in the input.

What differentiates CapsNets from traditional CNNs is the way in which capsules communicate with each other. During the process of training, CapsNets use a routing algorithm, called "Dynamic Routing," to find the best combination of capsules that agree on the instantiation parameters of the same feature. This routing algorithm is designed to generate a weighted sum of the predictions of different capsules based on the agreement between them. Capsules that agree well are given a higher weight, while those that do not agree are given a lower weight. This allows the network to dynamically route information between capsules that are more likely to be relevant to each other, and avoids the need for explicit max-pooling or neural layers, which are often used in CNNs to downsample feature maps.

Implementing CapsNets in Keras can be done using the Keras Capsule Layer API, which was introduced as part of Keras 2.0. This layer provides an easy way to specify the input shape, output dimensions, and number of capsules for each layer. One example of a CapsNet architecture in Keras is presented below:

```
from keras import layers, models

input_shape = (28, 28, 1)
num_classes = 10

# define the model architecture
model = models.Sequential()
model.add(layers.Conv2D(32, (3, 3), activation='relu', input_shape=input_shape))
model.add(layers.BatchNormalization())
model.add(layers.Conv2D(64, (3, 3), activation='relu'))
model.add(layers.BatchNormalization())
model.add(layers.Conv2D(128, (3, 3), activation='relu'))
model.add(layers.BatchNormalization())
model.add(layers.Conv2D(256, (3, 3), activation='relu'))
model.add(layers.BatchNormalization())
model.add(layers.Reshape(target_shape=(-1, 256)))
model.add(layers.Capsule(num_capsule=num_classes,
```

```
                          dim_capsule=16,
                          routings=3,
                          share_weights=True))
model.add(layers.Flatten())
model.add(layers.Dense(128, activation='relu'))
model.add(layers.Dropout(0.5))
model.add(layers.Dense(num_classes, activation='softmax'))

# compile the model
model.compile(loss='categorical_crossentropy',
              optimizer='adam',
              metrics=['accuracy'])
```

In this example, we define a CapsNet model for classification on the MNIST dataset. We start with a series of Conv2D and BatchNormalization layers to extract high-level features from the input images, followed by a Capsule layer with 10 capsules (one for each class) that is responsible for predicting the presence of each digit. This is then flattened and passed through a few fully connected layers before reaching the final output layer.

Overall, Capsule Networks are a promising development in the field of deep learning that offer several advantages over traditional CNNs, including improved robustness, generalization, and interpretability. They are easy to implement in Keras and are worth exploring for any project that involves image or speech processing.

5.19 What are some best practices for managing the lifecycle of a Keras model, from development to deployment and maintenance?

Managing the lifecycle of a Keras model can be challenging, especially if you're working on a large and complex project. However, there are some best practices you can follow to make the process smoother and more efficient.

1. Version Control: Always track and save versions of your Keras model during the development process. Version control software like Git can be used to keep track of changes, allowing you to roll back to any previous version of your model when necessary.

2. Modularity: Break your Keras model down into separate modules or components that correspond to different parts of the neural network. This makes it easier to manage, update and test the model as a whole.

3. Testing: Test your Keras models thoroughly before deploying them to ensure that they are accurate and robust. Implement automated tests to catch any issues that arise over the lifecycle of the project.

4. Deployment: Use containerization tools like Docker to deploy your Keras models in a consistent and reproducible way across multiple environments. Docker allows you to package your code and dependencies into a container and then deploy it to various production environments.

5. Monitoring: Monitor the performance of your Keras model in production to identify any issues or bugs. Use tools like TensorBoard to visualize training and validation metrics to verify if the model has good performance over time.

6. Caching: Consider caching the predictions of your Keras model to speed up your application. Predictions can be cached on every user request and serve the same prediction that was made before, thus reducing the load on your servers.

7. Optimization: Optimize your Keras model by using specific hardware or software accelerators such as NVIDIA GPUs or TPU. This may require additional development effort but can lead to significantly better performance.

Overall, following these best practices can help ensure that your Keras model is accurately developed, thoroughly tested, seamlessly deployed, and easily maintained throughout its lifecycle.

5.20   How do you evaluate the fairness and ethical considerations of a Keras model, and what are some techniques to mitigate potential biases in model predictions?

Evaluating the fairness and ethical considerations of a Keras model is crucial to ensure that the model does not perpetuate biased or discriminatory decisions. Here are some techniques to evaluate and mitigate potential biases in Keras model predictions:

1. Evaluate model performance across different groups: One way to assess the fairness of a model is to test its performance across different demographic or social groups. For example, if a model is used to make loan approval decisions, we can evaluate the model's accuracy for different ethnic or gender groups, ensuring it is not biased towards any particular group.

2. Check for input data biases: Training data biases can also play a role in a models output. Therefore, it is essential to perform data analysis to ensure that the training data set more fairly represents the real world. This requires checking for any biases in the data, such as under-representation of certain demographic groups or input data correlations that might impact model predictions. Real-world data might also create biases since it reflects historical biases, therefore careful down-sampling is needed to balance opportunities evenly.

3. Use Fairness Metrics: In machine learning, fairness metrics are used to measure the fairness of a model's predictions. These metrics evaluate the model's decision-making process and help identify any group-oriented biases in the model. Metrics such as equalized odds or demographic parity measure performance for the target variable based on subgroups by race, gender, and other factors.

4. Adjust Model Hyper-Parameters: Model builders should consider adjusting model parameters that may lead to model bias. Model builders should consider altering model parameters to mitigate model bias if the evaluation indicates that model bias exists.

5. Create transparent models: Transparent models such as linear

regression or decision tree models can help explain how the model decision-making process works. Transparent models can boost transparency by explaining the variables and variables contribution in the decision-making process.

6. Enforce regular model training: Enforcing regular model training helps ensure that the model remains updated on the latest data and does not retain outdated biases.

In conclusion, Keras models' bias and exclusion can continue to propagate unfairness and discrimination beyond human social and historical biases Which is why instead of isolating the data, we must attempt to eliminate potential model biases by making the model building process open, public and ethically evaluated.

Chapter 6

Guru

6.1 Can you discuss the challenges and limitations of the current Keras API in the context of emerging deep learning research trends and new architectures?

Keras is a widely used high-level deep learning framework that provides a user-friendly interface to build, train, and optimize deep neural networks. While Keras is capable of supporting a vast range of neural network architectures and research trends, there are still some limitations and challenges that need to be addressed.

In terms of limitations, Keras primarily relies on TensorFlow, Theano, or CNTK as the backend, which limits its cross-platform compatibility. As a result, models created using Keras may require additional modifications to work with other platforms or hardware. Additionally, Keras has a limited set of built-in data augmentation functions, which can be challenging when it comes to data preprocessing in specific research domains.

Another limitation is that Keras has relatively less support for integrations with external libraries, such as image processing tools and natural language processing libraries. This can be a limitation when working on complex projects, as it may require more time and effort to integrate these libraries into the Keras pipeline.

In terms of challenges, emerging deep learning research trends such as attention mechanisms, graph neural networks, and adversarial learning require significant modifications to the current Keras API. This can result in higher development times and efforts for researchers who want to experiment with these architectures using Keras. As these architectures continue to gain popularity in the research community, Keras will require significant developments and updates to provide support for these emerging trends.

To overcome these limitations and challenges, the Keras community and developers are continually working on updates and improvements to the API. For example, Keras has integrated support for TPUs (Tensor Processing Units) and added new modules such as the TensorFlow Datasets module to make data preprocessing easier. Additionally, Keras has also made efforts to integrate with external libraries for image processing and NLP.

In conclusion, while the current Keras API may have some limitations and challenges when it comes to supporting emerging trends and architectures, the support from the Keras community and developers, coupled with the flexibility and modularity of the framework, will continue to make it a viable choice for deep learning researchers and practitioners.

6.2   What are some key considerations for designing and implementing custom training algorithms in Keras that efficiently leverage the underlying hardware capabilities?

When designing custom training algorithms in Keras, there are several key considerations that should be taken into account in order to optimize for efficient utilization of underlying hardware capabilities.

Some of these considerations are:

1. Batch sizes - Deep learning models require processing large amounts of data, and by batching data, it's possible to take advantage of parallel computing capabilities of modern CPUs, GPUs, and TPUs. A small batch size can result in a slow training process because of the overhead of queuing the operations on the processor. It's typically recommended to use larger batch sizes for modern hardware, which can process multiple samples simultaneously and hence speed up the training process. However, using larger batch sizes may impact generalization or accuracy sometimes, so it is recommended to tune the batch size for optimal performance and acceptable loss in accuracy.

2. Data format - The hardware capabilities depend on the data format used by the model. Keras supports three possible configurations: channel-last, channel-first, and mixed. In channel-last, the input data is organized in such a way that the color channels are the last dimension, e.g. (batch_size, height, width, channels). This format is more memory-efficient and works better with vectorized GPU computations. Further, in cases where image inputs are of varying height and width and may need to be padded, this format is preferred. In channel-first format, the input data organize the color channels as the first dimension, e.g. (batch_size, channels, height, width). This format is more commonly used in older hardware configurations. Finally, the mixed data format enables your model to learn both spatial features as well as channel-related features parallelly.

3. Parallelism and hardware support Advances in specialized hardware for deep learning such as GPUs and TPUs, as well as Intel's OpenVino library, allows for accelerated computations during model training. In order to leverage this hardware support while training, Keras allows for the selection of parallelism options like CPU, single or multi-GPU, and TPUs, which varies depending on hardware availability and suitability.

4. Model Optimization Another crucial consideration is model optimization. Keras allows applying several optimization techniques like kernel regularizers, dropout, early stopping, batch normalization, and learning rate schedules. Selection of appropriate optimizer, regularization options, and so on is essential in achieving the best model efficiency.

5. Hardware-aware data processing In cases where Tensor Processing Units (TPU) can be utilized, the way the data is preprocessed and how the model is constructed can affect training performance. It is recommended that preprocessing steps such as tokenization and padding be performed on the device where the training will occur. This will speed up training and utilize the hardware capabilities at their best.

In summary, designing and implementing custom training algorithms in Keras requires careful consideration of the hardware capabilities and the overall goal of the model performance. Tensor Processing Units (TPUs), GPUs, and other specialized hardware can significantly speed up training, and implementing careful modeling, data formatting and preprocessing, and tuning of parallelism and optimization strategies can further enhance the model efficiency.

6.3   How do you adapt Keras to leverage emerging hardware architectures, such as neuromorphic computing or quantum computing platforms, for deep learning tasks?

Adapting Keras to leverage emerging hardware architectures for deep learning can be challenging since the traditional deep learning architectures may not be optimized for the new hardware.

First, it is essential to understand the hardware architecture to be used and identify the unique features and limitations that affect deep learning tasks. The neuromorphic computing architecture, for example, is designed to emulate the structure and function of the human brain, resulting in low power consumption and high processing speed. On the other hand, quantum computing platforms leverage quantum mechanics to provide faster and more efficient processing of complex problems.

Once you understand the hardware architecture, you can follow the steps outlined below to adapt Keras for deep learning tasks:

1. Implement custom layers: Keras allows users to create custom layers that can be added to existing neural network architectures. By implementing layers optimized for neuromorphic or quantum computing platforms, users can optimize the network for better performance.

2. Update the backend engine: Keras is designed to run on different backend engines such as TensorFlow or Theano. To adapt Keras to a new hardware architecture, the backend engine must be updated to support the new hardware.

3. Optimize the network architecture: It is essential to optimize the network architecture to leverage the unique features and specifications of the new hardware. For example, quantum computing platforms require the use of quantum algorithms that can exploit the properties of quantum systems for faster computation.

4. Compile and train the model: Once the network architecture has been optimized, the Keras model must be compiled and trained on the new hardware. This step may require specialized hardware programming languages or frameworks, such as Qiskit for quantum computing.

5. Evaluate performance: After training the model, it is important to evaluate its performance and compare it with existing deep learning architectures to determine the effectiveness of the adaptation.

One example of adapting Keras to emerging hardware architecture is the implementation of the NEST (neural simulation tool) framework on specialized neuromorphic computing hardware. This allowed researchers to exploit the unique features of the neuromorphic hardware to achieve better performance in their deep learning tasks.

In conclusion, adapting Keras for emerging hardware architectures requires a deep understanding of the target architecture and its unique features. By implementing custom layers, updating the backend engine, optimizing the network architecture, and evaluating the performance, users can leverage the benefits of these emerging technologies to improve deep learning tasks.

6.4 Can you explain the trade-offs involved in designing a scalable and maintainable deep learning system architecture that combines Keras with other components, such as data processing pipelines and model serving infrastructure?

Designing a scalable and maintainable deep learning system architecture involves balancing multiple trade-offs. One major trade-off is the trade-off between flexibility and complexity.

On one hand, a flexible architecture should accommodate a wide range of model types and data sources. For example, it should allow for changes in data preprocessing, augmentation, and feature engineering. Keras is a highly flexible deep learning framework that enables users to build and train a wide variety of models using a range of network architectures and optimization algorithms. To ensure flexibility, the design should allow for modularization and easy component swapping.

However, flexibility can come at the cost of complexity. The more components you add to a system, the harder it generally becomes to maintain and scale. Therefore, we need to consider the complexity of maintaining the system. In order to alleviate complexity, one can opt for a simpler architecture where Keras is combined with other specialized and complementary components.

For example, data processing pipelines (such as Apache Beam or Apache Nifi) can be used to extract, transform, and load data into the system. These pipelines allow the data to be cleaned, transformed, and enriched before training the model. This approach could help to keep the data management and processing separate from the model training, which can be valuable in a number of use cases.

Another potential component to consider is the model serving infrastructure. After the model has been trained, it needs to be deployed to serve real-time predictions in production. For this purpose, there are specialized serving systems one can incorporate such as Tensor-Flow Serving or Seldon Core. These can handle the complexities of load-balancing, scaling, and versioning of the model.

In conclusion, a scalable and maintainable architecture that combines Keras with other components, such as data processing pipelines and model serving infrastructure, involves balancing the trade-offs between flexibility, complexity, and maintainability. By identifying a manageable number of specialized components that integrate easily with each other, we can establish a scalable and flexible pipeline for deep learning models that is easier to maintain over time.

6.5 How can Keras be integrated with other machine learning frameworks or libraries to enable more effective multi-framework workflows and facilitate collaboration across different research communities?

Keras is a popular open-source deep learning library that aims to provide a user-friendly interface to build and train deep learning models. Keras is built on top of other backend deep learning frameworks such as TensorFlow, Theano, and CNTK. This makes it easy to integrate Keras with other machine learning frameworks and libraries, enabling more effective multi-framework workflows and facilitating collaboration across different research communities.

Here are some ways to integrate Keras with other machine learning frameworks or libraries:

1. Use Keras with TensorFlow: TensorFlow is the most popular backend of Keras. Keras abstracts the low-level details of TensorFlow and makes it easier for users to build and train deep learning models. Keras also provides a rich set of functionality for data preprocessing and model evaluation. You can use the high-level APIs of Keras and the low-level APIs of TensorFlow together to build complex models.

2. Use Keras with PyTorch: PyTorch is another popular deep learning framework that provides dynamic computation graphs, which allows you to change the computational graph on-the-fly during training. Keras can be used as a wrapper around PyTorch models, providing a high-level API for data preprocessing, model building, and model evaluation.

3. Use Keras with scikit-learn: Scikit-learn is a popular machine learning library in Python that provides a wide range of tools for data preprocessing, feature selection, and model evaluation. Keras can be used in conjunction with scikit-learn for deep learning tasks. For example, you can use scikit-learn to preprocess data and Keras to build and train deep learning models.

4. Use Keras with Apache Spark: Apache Spark is a popular distributed computing framework that can be used for big data processing. Keras can be used with Apache Spark to build and train deep learning models on large datasets. You can use Spark to distribute the preprocessing of large datasets and Keras to build and train deep learning models.

Integrating Keras with other machine learning frameworks or libraries can improve the flexibility and efficiency of your workflow. It can also enable collaboration across different research communities and facilitate the development of new techniques and methods.

6.6   Can you discuss the role of Keras in the development and standardization of new deep learning and machine learning benchmarks, as well as the evaluation of new model architectures and training techniques?

Keras has played a significant role in the development and standardization of new deep learning and machine learning benchmarks, as well as the evaluation of new model architectures and training techniques. Let me explain why.

First, Keras provides a user-friendly, high-level API for building and training neural networks. This makes it easy for researchers to experiment with new network architectures and training techniques, allowing them to quickly prototype and evaluate ideas.

Second, Keras has become a de facto industry standard for deep learning. The framework has been widely adopted by both researchers and practitioners, making it easier to compare and reproduce results across different studies and applications.

Third, Keras provides a wide range of pre-trained models and tools for transfer learning, which can be used to benchmark new model architectures and training techniques against existing state-of-the-art approaches.

Fourth, Keras has a growing community of developers and users, who are actively contributing new models, datasets, and evaluation metrics. This community-driven approach helps to ensure that benchmarks are up-to-date and relevant, and that the framework remains at the forefront of deep learning research and development.

Overall, Keras has played a pivotal role in both the development and standardization of new deep learning and machine learning benchmarks, as well as the evaluation of new model architectures and training techniques. Its ease-of-use, popularity, and community-driven approach have made it an invaluable tool for researchers and practitioners alike.

6.7   What are some key challenges in developing a more unified and extensible Keras API that can support a broader range of deep learning tasks, including unsupervised, self-supervised, and reinforcement learning?

Keras has become a popular high-level deep learning API due to its user-friendly interface and ease of use. However, as the field of deep

learning evolves, there is a growing need to support a broader range
of tasks, including unsupervised, self-supervised, and reinforcement
learning. There are several key challenges in developing a more unified
and extensible Keras API to support these tasks:

1. Model Architecture Flexibility: Keras is known for its layer-by-
layer approach, and the current architecture is highly dependent on
the specific task at hand. Extending this architecture approach to
tasks that don't fit neatly into this paradigm, such as those requiring complex recurrent architectures, requires a more flexible model
architecture definition process.

2. Portability: Given most deep learning frameworks' highly specialized and unique APIs, developers invest a considerable amount
of time learning the framework. Ensuring portability across deep
learning frameworks requires abstracting the differences between the
targeted frameworks so they can operate uniformly.

3. Intuitive API: Machine learning users come from a wide range
of backgrounds, most notably in engineering domains. Therefore,
it is imperative that Keras's API be intuitive and easy to learn to
encourage future innovation.

4. Scalability: Many tasks like self-supervised learning require enor-
mous amounts of data. Therefore, scalability is essential, and the support for distributed training and the flexible architecure mentioned
before goes a long way to achieving this.

5. Lack of Standardization: The deep learning field is still relatively
young, and there is a general lack of standardization in approaches
and methods. As a result, offering extensibility requires compromise
and balancing of best practices and cooperation with other frameworks to produce a standardized deep learning workflow.

To address these challenges, the Keras development team has taken
various steps, including:

1. Integrating key functionality directly into Keras, such as Tensor-
Flow Probability for probabilistic approaches.

2. Collaborating with other frameworks and industry leaders to establish best practices and ensure future compatibility.

3. Offering custom layer and model classes to enable more flexibility in Keras's model architecture.

4. Designing more modular and pluggable APIs so developers can modify, extend and reimagine existing components without the need for core changes.

5. Progressively adding to the API with new building blocks, such as the recent addition of the transformers module targeting long-context NLP tasks.

Overall, although Keras has enjoyed considerable success, the challenges in developing a more unified and extensible API that supports a broader range of deep learning tasks will not be solved overnight, and the team behind Keras will continue to work tirelessly in that direction.

6.8 How can Keras be adapted to support more advanced optimization techniques, such as second-order optimization methods, that may offer improved convergence properties and better generalization performance?

Keras provides an easy-to-use and high-level API for building deep neural network models. However, it may not always support advanced optimization techniques out of the box that could improve the performance of the model. In this case, you can customize the optimization process by creating a custom optimizer that utilizes advanced optimization techniques, such as second-order optimization methods.

Here are the steps you can follow to create a custom optimizer in Keras:

1. Define the optimizer class: First, you need to define the new optimizer class by inheriting the base optimizer class from Keras ('keras.optimizers.Optimizer'). This class should implement the '__init__'

and 'get_updates' methods.

2. Implement the '__init__' method: In the '__init__' method, you should define any additional hyperparameters for the optimizer, such as the learning rate, momentum, and decay rate.

3. Implement the 'get_updates' method: In the 'get_updates' method, you should define the optimization algorithm. This method should return a list of update operations that update the weights of the neural network.

4. Compile the model with the custom optimizer: Once you've defined the custom optimizer class, you can use it to compile your Keras model. You can do this by passing an instance of the custom optimizer class to the 'compile' method of the model.

Here is an example of creating a custom optimizer that utilizes the L-BFGS optimization algorithm, a second-order optimization method:

```
import keras.backend as K
from keras.optimizers import Optimizer

class LBFGS(Optimizer):
    def __init__(self, max_iter=20, **kwargs):
        super(LBFGS, self).__init__(**kwargs)
        self.max_iter = max_iter

    def get_updates(self, params, constraints, loss):
        grads = self.get_gradients(loss, params)
        updates = []
        memory = [K.zeros(K.int_shape(p)) for p in params]
        old_grads = [K.zeros(K.int_shape(p)) for p in params]
        yk = None

        for i in range(self.max_iter):
            # Compute the gradient
            g = [grads[j] + self.beta * old_grads[j] for j in range(len(params))
]

            # Compute the search direction
            if yk is not None:
                pk = K.tf.scalar_mul(-1, g)
                uk = [K.tf.reduce_sum(memory[j] * g[j]) for j in range(len(
params))]
                pk = [pk[i] + uk[i] * yk for i in range(len(params))]
            else:
                pk = K.tf.scalar_mul(-1, g)

            # Define the loss and update steps
            loss = K.tf.reduce_mean(loss)
            updates.append([memory[i], memory[i] + K.square(g[i]) for i in range
(len(params))])
                updates.append([old_grads[i], g[i] for i in range(len(params))])
                updates.append([params[i], params[i] + self.lr * pk[i] for i in
range(len(params))])

                # Compute the new gradient and yk
                new_grads = self.get_gradients(loss, params)
```

```
        sk = [params[i] - memory[i] for i in range(len(params))]
        yk = [new_grads[i] - grads[i] for i in range(len(params))]
        yk = [yk[i] - K.tf.scalar_mul(K.tf.reduce_sum(memory[j] * yk[j]), sk
[i]) for i in range(len(params))]
        yk = [K.tf.scalar_mul(1 / K.tf.reduce_sum(K.square(sk[i])), yk[i])
for i in range(len(params))]

        # Update the gradient and old_grads
        grads = new_grads
        old_grads = g

    return updates
```

In the above example, we defined the 'get_updates' method to use the L-BFGS optimization algorithm. We also used the '__init__' method to set the maximum number of iterations and other hyper-parameters of the optimizer.

Once you've defined the optimizer class, you can use it to compile your Keras model:

```
from keras.models import Sequential
from keras.layers import Dense

model = Sequential()
model.add(Dense(10, input_dim=784, activation='relu'))
model.add(Dense(1, activation='sigmoid'))

optimizer = LBFGS()
model.compile(loss='binary_crossentropy', optimizer=optimizer)
```

In this example, we passed an instance of the 'LBFGS' optimizer class to the 'compile' method of the Keras model. The model will now use the custom optimizer during training, which should lead to better convergence and generalization performance.

6.9   What are some key considerations when implementing privacy-preserving techniques, such as federated learning or differential privacy, in Keras to ensure that models can be trained and deployed in sensitive or regulated environments?

When implementing privacy-preserving techniques, such as federated learning or differential privacy, in Keras to ensure that models can be trained and deployed in sensitive or regulated environments, it is important to consider the following key factors:

1. Data Privacy: The privacy of the data used to train the models is of utmost importance. Ensure that the data is protected at all times and that access to the data is strictly controlled. For example, in the case of federated learning, data should be encrypted during transmission and training should be done on the device or server where it originates.

2. Model Privacy: When deploying models, it's important to ensure that the model architecture and the weights are protected from reverse engineering or tampering. This can be achieved through techniques such as model encryption or obfuscation of layers.

3. Model Robustness: It's important to ensure that the privacy-preserving techniques used do not compromise the accuracy or robustness of the model. For example, in the case of differential privacy, adding too much noise to the training data can reduce model accuracy.

4. Regulatory Compliance: In regulated environments, it's important to ensure compliance with legal or regulatory requirements. For example, in the healthcare industry, models must comply with HIPAA regulations protecting patient privacy.

5. Ethical Considerations: The potential impact of the model on society, fairness, and unintended consequences should be carefully evaluated. For example, models trained on biased data may perpetuate

discrimination.

Examples of these considerations in practice:

Federated Learning: In federated learning, data privacy is maintained by keeping user data on the device and training models on the device itself. The models are then aggregated on the server, without ever exposing the raw data. To ensure regulatory compliance, access control mechanisms can be implemented to limit access to the servers.

Differential Privacy: Differential privacy preserves data privacy by adding controlled noise to the training data to mask individual data points. However, the amount of noise added must be balanced with the accuracy of the model. For example, a company might choose to use differential privacy to train a recommendation system, but at the same time, must ensure that the recommended products are diverse and not biased.

Model Encryption: Model encryption can be used to protect model privacy by encrypting the model architecture and weights. This helps prevent reverse engineering or tampering. For example, in the case of financial industry models, it is legally required to protect the model IP from being stolen or compromised.

In summary, implementing privacy-preserving techniques in Keras requires careful consideration of all the above factors and is specific to unique privacy and regulatory requirements of each industry.

6.10   Can you discuss the role of Keras in enabling more effective collaboration between the deep learning research community and other scientific disciplines, such as neuroscience, cognitive science, and psychology, to advance our understanding of learning and intelligence?

Keras is a high-level neural network API written in Python that makes it easy to build and train deep learning models. One of the key benefits of Keras is its simplicity and ease of use, which has made it a popular tool among researchers and practitioners in a wide range of scientific disciplines, including neuroscience, cognitive science, and psychology.

One way that Keras has enabled more effective collaboration between the deep learning research community and other scientific disciplines is by providing a common language for describing and implementing deep learning architectures. This has made it easier for researchers from different fields to work together, share ideas, and build on each other's work.

For example, in neuroscience, Keras has been used to develop models that simulate neural activity and help researchers better understand how the brain works. These models can be trained on large datasets of neural activity and then used to make predictions about how the brain will respond to different stimuli.

Similarly, in cognitive science and psychology, Keras has been used to build models of human cognition and behavior. These models can be trained on behavioral data and then used to make predictions about how humans will respond in different situations. This has led to new insights into the underlying mechanisms of learning and intelligence, and has helped researchers develop more effective interventions for a variety of cognitive and psychological disorders.

In addition to its role in enabling collaboration between different scientific disciplines, Keras has also contributed to the democratization of deep learning. Its ease of use and accessibility have made it possible for researchers and practitioners from a wide range of backgrounds to build and train deep learning models, without requiring a deep understanding of the underlying mathematical concepts.

Overall, Keras has played an important role in advancing our understanding of learning and intelligence, by enabling more effective collaboration between the deep learning research community and other scientific disciplines. By providing a common language for describing and implementing deep learning architectures, and by making it easier for researchers to build and train models, Keras has helped to accelerate the pace of scientific discovery and innovation.

6.11 How can Keras be used to support research on the integration of symbolic reasoning and deep learning, enabling more powerful and interpretable models that can perform complex reasoning tasks?

Symbolic reasoning is the process of using logical deductions to solve problems or generate new information. Deep learning, on the other hand, is a type of artificial intelligence that learns from large amounts of data to make predictions and perform tasks. Combining these two areas has the potential to create powerful and interpretable models that can perform complex reasoning tasks.

Keras is a high-level neural network library built in Python that provides an easy-to-use interface for building and training deep learning models. It can be used to support research on the integration of symbolic reasoning and deep learning in several ways.

One way Keras can be used is by incorporating symbolic reasoning into the structure of a neural network. For example, researchers could add a symbolic reasoning module to a deep neural network that is trained on large amounts of data. The symbolic reasoning module could then use logical inferences to perform more complex reasoning tasks, such as answering questions or generating new information.

Another way Keras can be used to support this research is by providing a framework for experimenting with different architectures and algorithms. Researchers can use Keras to build and train deep learning models that incorporate symbolic reasoning, and then compare their performance with other models using standard evaluation metrics.

One example of using Keras for symbolic reasoning is the Neural Module Network (NMN) architecture. NMN is a neural network model that incorporates modules for symbolic reasoning, enabling it to perform complex tasks such as language understanding and question answering. NMN can be built and trained using Keras, and has shown promising results in several benchmarks.

Keras can also be used to create interpretable models that can explain how decisions are made. Researchers can incorporate techniques such as attention mechanisms, explainable AI (XAI), and saliency maps, to build models that provide clear and understandable explanations of how they arrived at their output.

In conclusion, Keras provides a flexible and powerful framework for researchers to integrate symbolic reasoning into deep learning. By incorporating symbolic reasoning into the structure of deep neural networks, researchers can create more powerful and interpretable models that can perform complex reasoning tasks.

6.12 What are some key challenges and best practices for developing and maintaining a large-scale, production-ready Keras codebase that can support the rapid iteration and deployment of new deep learning models and features?

Developing and maintaining a large-scale, production-ready Keras codebase can present several challenges, but the following are some of the most critical ones:

1. Data pipeline management: Developing a robust and efficient data pipeline is critical to success when dealing with large-scale Keras projects. The pipeline should be scalable so that it can handle any increase in the volume of data that the model processes. A well-designed pipeline should also be able to preprocess and clean up data as it comes in (normalization, data augmentation, etc.) and to enable smooth implementation of new data sources.

2. Performance optimization: Large-scale Keras projects can be time-consuming, and model training and inference can take a lot of time when processing large data sets. It is essential to optimize data processing and model training times to ensure that a smooth iteration is possible.

3. Model monitoring: As the number of models in the codebase increases, it is critical to ensure that each model is performing well and is within the threshold set for accuracy, training time, and resource usage. Proper model monitoring is essential to track performance over time and to identify when a model might need to be re-trained or retired.

4. Versioning: Effective version control is necessary to keep track of changes that are made to models, datasets, and the project's codebase. Proper version control enables efficient collaboration among team members and helps avoid conflicts and regressions.

To address these challenges, we recommend the following best practices:

1. Use modular code: To make your code more manageable and scalable, break it up into smaller, more manageable modules. This strategy will allow for easier model iteration, testing and deployment. When new features are implemented, they can be tested and deployed independently of other features, making it easier to detect any issues during the iteration process.

2. Use cloud computing resources: By using cloud computing solutions like Google Cloud Platform, Amazon Web Services or Microsoft Azure, you can scale processing resources and storage to handle big data sets and improve the speed of the data processing and model training.

3. Use data augmentation: Data augmentation is an essential technique for creating more diverse training data sets by applying various preprocessing techniques such as rotation, scaling, flipping, and so on. This can enable the model to learn better and generalize to emerging patterns.

4. Use transfer learning: Transfer learning is a technique where a pre-trained neural network model is used to train new models for the required tasks. It allows starting from a pre-trained model with existing features learned through a vast data pool on a specific domain, which in turn transfers that knowledge to a new task.

5. Implement continuous integration: Continuous integration and testing enable efficient and rapid testing and deployment of models, as well as quick identification of issues as they surface. Developers run tests automatically to check new codebase changes to ensure that the overall system functions appropriately.

6. Follow the latest best practices and advances: The field of deep learning is continually evolving, and best practices and state-of-the-art techniques are always emerging. It is important to stay up-to-date, so you can implement new features, technologies, and processes that can improve your model and make it more efficient and accurate.

Overall, developing and managing a production-ready Keras codebase requires careful planning, attention to best practices, and a focus on scalability, robustness, performance, and monitoring. By following these guidelines and strategies, you will be better equipped to manage large-scale projects with a high level of efficiency and effectiveness.

6.13 How can Keras be extended to support emerging research areas, such as learning with less data, transfer learning across domains or tasks, or learning in adversarial environments, where traditional deep learning approaches may struggle?

Keras can be extended to support emerging research areas by implementing new layers, loss functions, and metrics, as well as developing new algorithms that address the unique challenges of these research areas. For example:

1. Learning with less data: This research area is focused on developing algorithms that can learn from small amounts of data, such as few-shot learning, one-shot learning, and zero-shot learning. To extend Keras for these tasks, new layers that allow for flexible input shapes and sizes can be implemented, such as convolutional neural networks (CNNs) that can take in images of varying sizes. Additionally, transfer learning techniques, such as fine-tuning pre-trained networks or learning representations across multiple tasks, can be utilized to improve performance with limited data.

2. Transfer learning across domains or tasks: Transfer learning is the process of leveraging knowledge learned in one domain or task to improve performance in a new, related domain or task. Extending Keras to support transfer learning involves building pre-trained models on large, diverse datasets and providing implementations of various transfer learning methods, such as fine-tuning, adaptation, and multi-task learning. Furthermore, new metrics that evaluate the transferability of learned features and architectures can be created.

3. Learning in adversarial environments: Adversarial learning is the process of training models to be robust against attacks or adversarial examples. Defense mechanisms such as adversarial training and robust optimization can be implemented in Keras to improve model robustness. Additionally, new loss functions that incorporate adversarial objectives, such as minimizing the worst-case loss or maximizing

predictive uncertainty, can be designed.

In order to extend Keras for these research areas, it is important
to first understand the unique challenges and requirements of each
problem. This often requires a deep understanding of the specific
problem domain, as well as knowledge of recent research advances
and techniques. By implementing new features and algorithms that
address these challenges, Keras can continue to be a valuable tool for
researchers and practitioners in the deep learning community.

6.14 What are some key considerations for adapting Keras to support more advanced model architectures and learning paradigms, such as dynamic computation graphs, differentiable programming, or neuro-symbolic architectures?

To adapt Keras to support more advanced model architectures and
learning paradigms, there are several key considerations to keep in
mind:

1. Compatibility with existing Keras code: If you are adapting Keras
to support new features, it is important to maintain compatibility
with existing Keras code and functionality. This will ensure that
users can easily transition to the new features without having to re-
learn everything from scratch.

2. Scalability: As models become more complex, it is important to
ensure that Keras can scale to cope with larger models and datasets.
This means optimizing the implementation to run efficiently on the
available hardware, and leveraging distributed computing techniques
where necessary.

3. Flexibility: To support dynamic computation graphs and other
advanced model architectures, Keras needs to be flexible enough to
support different types of data flows, dynamic model construction,

and complex layer types. For example, dynamic models might require different APIs for building layers, while differentiable programming might require custom loss functions or other specialized functions.

4. Interoperability: To support neuro-symbolic architectures, Keras can benefit from interoperability with other tools and libraries, such as tensor flow or PyTorch. This allows users to harness the strengths of different tools and combine them effectively in a single workflow.

5. Community support: Lastly, to be successful in supporting more advanced model architectures and learning paradigms, Keras will need to build an active and supportive community of developers and users who can contribute improvements and share knowledge about how to use Keras effectively. This means actively engaging users through forums, blogs, and other channels, and promoting open collaboration and sharing of code and resources.

In terms of specific examples, one way to support dynamic computation graphs might be to introduce a new API for building layers that is more flexible and expressive than the current static API. This might involve adding new functions for building dynamic models that support variable-length inputs or outputs, as well as functions for constructing and connecting layers dynamically at runtime.

For differentiable programming, Keras might need to add support for custom loss functions or gradients that can be optimized using gradient descent. This might involve exposing lower-level APIs for building custom loss functions or gradients, and providing ways to integrate these functions with other Keras components.

Finally, for neuro-symbolic architectures, Keras might benefit from interoperability with other libraries used in neuro-symbolic AI such as NLP libraries, which can be used to model symbolic knowledge, and integration with symbolic reasoning systems to build hybrid models that incorporate both neural networks and symbolic reasoning.

6.15   Can you discuss the role of Keras in advancing the state of the art in deep learning-based natural language processing, computer vision, and other application domains, as well as the key challenges and opportunities in these areas?

Keras is a popular open-source deep learning library that allows researchers and developers to quickly prototype and build deep learning models. Keras offers a user-friendly interface that simplifies the process of building, training, and deploying deep learning models. With Keras, researchers and developers can easily experiment and iterate on deep learning models and quickly make progress in developing state-of-the-art models for natural language processing, computer vision, and other domains.

In natural language processing, Keras has played a significant role in advancing the state of the art in a variety of tasks such as language modeling, text classification, named entity recognition, and machine translation. For example, by using Keras and deep learning, researchers have been able to develop language models that can generate human-like text and conversational agents that can understand and generate responses to human language. Additionally, Keras has enabled the development of deep learning models that are capable of understanding the semantic meaning of text by leveraging pre-trained word embeddings.

In computer vision, Keras has enabled researchers and developers to develop highly accurate and efficient deep learning models for tasks such as object detection, image classification, face recognition, and semantic segmentation. Keras offers an extensive collection of pre-trained models such as VGG, ResNet, and Inception, which can be fine-tuned on specific tasks with small datasets, enabling researchers and developers to quickly develop state-of-the-art models even with limited data.

Despite the significant progress made in natural language processing, computer vision, and other domains using deep learning and Keras, there are still significant challenges that the community faces. For example, one significant challenge is developing models that can generalize to unseen data, especially in cases where the distribution of data is significantly different from the training data. Another challenge is developing models that are robust to adversarial attacks and can maintain high accuracy even when the input is slightly perturbed.

Overall, Keras has been instrumental in advancing the state of the art in deep learning-based natural language processing, computer vision, and other domains. With its user-friendly interface and extensive pre-trained models, Keras has enabled researchers and developers to easily experiment and iterate on deep learning models, leading to significant progress in these fields. However, there are still significant challenges to be addressed to enable even greater progress in these areas.

6.16 How can Keras be used to develop more robust and reliable deep learning models that can effectively handle uncertainty, noise, or distribution shifts in the input data, or that can be more easily verified and validated?

Keras is a powerful deep learning framework that provides various capabilities to develop robust and reliable models using different techniques. Here are several ways Keras can be used to achieve this goal:

1. Regularization: Regularization is one of the most popular techniques used to develop more robust models in machine learning. In Keras, different types of regularization techniques such as L1, L2, and dropout are available to prevent overfitting of the model. By applying regularization techniques, the model can learn more robust features and generalize better to new data.

2. Data Augmentation: Data augmentation is a technique that gener-

ates new training data by applying different transformations such as
rotations, scaling, and flipping to the existing data. This technique
is useful when training data is limited, and it helps in preventing
overfitting of the model.

3. Ensemble Learning: Ensemble learning is a technique that combines predictions from multiple models to make better predictions. In
Keras, we can develop multiple models and combine their predictions
to achieve better performance, and this approach provides robustness
to model predictions.

4. Bayesian Optimization: Bayesian optimization is a technique for
hyperparameter tuning that allows the model to quickly converge on
the optimal set of hyperparameters. Keras provides a useful library,
Kerastuner, that can be used to perform Bayesian optimization for
hyperparameter tuning.

5. Out-of-Distribution Detection: Out-of-distribution (OOD) detection is an essential component of model reliability. In Keras, we can
use techniques such as uncertainty quantification to identify samples
in the test set that are not similar to the training data. By identifying and removing these samples from the test set, we can improve
the reliability of the model.

6. Model Explainability: Model explainability helps in understanding
the model's decision-making process by identifying important features
used by the model to make predictions. In Keras, we can use techniques such as saliency maps and Grad-CAM to understand how the
model makes predictions.

7. Model Verification: Model verification is an important aspect of
model development, especially in critical applications such as healthcare and finance. In Keras, we can use techniques such as model
interpretability and adversarial testing to verify the model's correct-
ness and robustness.

In summary, Keras provides various techniques for developing robust
and reliable deep learning models that can handle uncertainty, noise,
or distribution shifts in the input data. By applying these techniques,
we can develop models that generalize better to new data and provide
better performance on unseen data.

6.17 What are some key challenges and opportunities in using Keras to develop more energy-efficient deep learning models and training algorithms that can help address the growing computational and environmental costs of deep learning research and deployment?

There are several challenges and opportunities in using Keras to develop more energy-efficient deep learning models and training algorithms that can help address the growing computational and environmental costs of deep learning research and deployment. Here are a few of them:

1. Challenge: Balancing computation and accuracy.

Opportunity: Keras provides a simple and user-friendly platform to experiment with different architectures and optimization techniques to find the right balance between computation and accuracy. Researchers can use Keras to quickly prototype different models and compare their performance in terms of accuracy and computational efficiency. For example, techniques like pruning and quantization can be used to reduce the computation while still maintaining high accuracy. Keras has built-in support for pruning and quantization, making it easier for researchers to experiment with these techniques.

2. Challenge: Minimizing power consumption.

Opportunity: Keras allows researchers to experiment with different optimization techniques that can reduce the power consumption of deep learning models. For example, techniques like batch normalization and weight decay can be used to reduce the number of computations required during training, which can result in lower power consumption. Keras has built-in support for these techniques, making it easier for researchers to experiment with them.

3. Challenge: Optimizing hardware for deep learning.

Opportunity: Keras provides an abstraction layer between the deep learning models and the hardware. This makes it easier to optimize the hardware for deep learning. For example, Keras models can be easily ported to specialized hardware like GPUs, TPUs, and FPGAs. This can result in significant improvements in performance and power efficiency. Keras also has support for distributed training, allowing researchers to scale their models across multiple devices.

4. Challenge: Addressing environmental concerns.

Opportunity: With the growing concerns about the environmental impact of deep learning, there is an opportunity to use Keras to develop more environmentally friendly models and training algorithms. This can be achieved by using techniques like knowledge distillation and transfer learning, which can reduce the amount of data and computation required during training, resulting in lower energy consumption. Keras has built-in support for these techniques, making it easier for researchers to experiment with them.

In summary, using Keras to develop more energy-efficient deep learning models and training algorithms can help address the growing computational and environmental costs of deep learning research and deployment. Keras provides a user-friendly platform to experiment with different architectures and optimization techniques, allowing researchers to find the right balance between computation and accuracy, minimize power consumption, optimize hardware, and address environmental concerns.

6.18 How can Keras support research on more biologically plausible deep learning models and learning algorithms that can shed light on the neural mechanisms underlying learning and cognition, and potentially lead to more powerful and efficient artificial systems?

Keras can support research on more biologically plausible deep learning models and algorithms in a number of ways.

First, Keras offers a flexible and easy-to-use framework for building neural networks with a variety of architectural choices, such as different types of layers and activation functions. This allows researchers to experiment with new types of models and algorithms that may better account for the mechanisms of learning in the brain.

Second, Keras includes a number of tools for implementing various types of regularization techniques, such as dropout and weight decay, which can be important for creating models that are more biologically plausible. For example, dropout can be used to model the stochastic nature of synaptic connections in the brain, while weight decay can be used to capture the effects of homeostatic mechanisms that regulate network activity.

Third, Keras can be used in conjunction with other tools and frameworks for simulating and analyzing neural activity, such as Neuromatch, Nengo, or the Neural Engineering Framework. These tools allow researchers to integrate neural simulations with deep learning models, and to investigate how different network architectures and learning algorithms might be more or less consistent with the known properties of biological neural circuits.

Fourth, Keras supports the use of transfer learning, which can be a powerful tool for building biologically realistic deep learning models. For example, researchers can use pre-trained models that have been trained on large-scale natural image datasets, and fine-tune them on more specialized biological datasets, such as images of neurons or brain scans. This approach can help ensure that the models use features and representations that are more consistent with the properties of biological systems.

Finally, Keras can be used in conjunction with other software tools for more detailed analysis of neural activity, such as spike sorting and calcium imaging. These tools can help researchers extract more precise information about the activity of individual neurons or small groups of neurons, which can in turn be used to guide the design and evaluation of deep learning models.

In summary, Keras can support research on more biologically plausible deep learning models and learning algorithms by providing a flexible and easy-to-use framework for building models, supporting regularization and transfer learning techniques, integrating with other tools for simulating and analyzing neural activity, and supporting more detailed analysis of individual neuron activity.

6.19   Can you discuss the role of Keras in the development and evaluation of novel deep learning-based approaches to unsolved or open-ended problems, such as artificial general intelligence, common sense reasoning, or creativity?

Keras can be an indispensable tool in the development and evaluation of novel deep learning-based approaches to unsolved or open-ended problems like artificial general intelligence (AGI), common sense reasoning, and creativity.

Firstly, Keras provides an array of pre-built and easily customizable neural network layers and models that are commonly used in these types of problems. For example, recurrent neural networks (RNNs), long short-term memory (LSTM) networks, and generative adversarial networks (GANs) are all regularly used in research relating to AGI, common sense reasoning, and creativity. Keras allows researchers to quickly and easily implement these neural network architectures while customizing them to the particular requirements of their research. This freedom to quickly prototype and test custom architectures allows researchers to experiment more freely and at a faster pace.

Secondly, Keras allows for easy integration with other Python libraries for tasks such as data manipulation and visualization. For example, Keras can be used in conjunction with TensorFlow to conduct training and evaluation on large datasets for AGI research. Similarly, Keras can be used alongside visualization libraries such as Matplotlib to display results in a useful and intuitive way.

Finally, Keras is designed to promote reproducibility. By providing a user-friendly and consistent interface to implement deep learning models, Keras makes it easier for researchers to share their models and results with others. This makes it much easier for others to replicate and extend this work, potentially advancing research in these fields more quickly.

In summary, the role of Keras in the development and evaluation of novel deep learning-based approaches to unsolved or open-ended problems such as AGI, common sense reasoning, or creativity is crucial. By providing researchers with pre-built neural network layers and models that are easily customizable, smooth integration with other Python libraries, and promoting reproducibility, Keras enables researchers to explore and experiment with these complex problems in a more efficient and effective way.

6.20   What are some key considerations for developing and maintaining a thriving open-source ecosystem around Keras, including fostering collaboration, ensuring reproducibility, and promoting the responsible and ethical use of deep learning technologies?

Developing and maintaining a thriving open-source ecosystem around Keras requires careful attention to a number of key considerations. In this response, I will discuss several strategies for fostering collaboration, ensuring reproducibility, and promoting responsible and ethical use of deep learning technologies.

1. Fostering collaboration:

One of the most important factors in building a thriving open-source ecosystem around Keras is to foster collaboration and engagement amongst contributors, users, and stakeholders. This can be achieved through a number of strategies, including:

- Encouraging contributions: One of the key ways to promote collaboration is to encourage contributions from the community. This can involve creating clear guidelines for submitting code, documentation, and other resources, as well as providing feedback and support for contributors. - Creating a welcoming community: Building a supportive and inclusive community is essential for success, so it's important to create a welcoming environment that encourages people to participate. This can involve setting clear expectations for behavior, providing resources for newcomers, and actively promoting positive interactions within the community. - Sponsoring events and initiatives: Sponsorships, such as hackathons, coding events, and mentorship programs, can also encourage collaboration by bringing people together to work on common goals.

2. Ensuring reproducibility:

Another important consideration is to ensure that projects developed with Keras are reproducible, meaning they can be replicated by others with similar results. This can involve a number of strategies, including:

- Documenting code: Clear and accessible documentation for your codebase can make it easier for others to reproduce your results. This can include documenting codebase structure, API usage, and mathematical models. - Making code available: By providing access to code, datasets and model checkpoints, users can reproduce previous results or models more easily. - Using version control: Using version control tools like Git, you can trace the evolution of the codebase over time, allowing others to identify any changes that could have affected the results.

3. Promoting responsible and ethical use of deep learning technologies:

Deep learning models have the potential to be used in a wide range of applications, from improving medical diagnosis to optimizing stock trading algorithms. However, because of their power and complexity, there is a need for ethical considerations as to their use. Here are some strategies to promote responsible and ethical use of Keras:

- Developing and adopting ethical guidelines: Clear guidelines or policies can help to guide developers and stakeholders in making responsible and ethical decisions around the use of deep learning technologies. - Consulting experts: Engaging with experts in the field, such as ethicists, advocacy groups, and policymakers can also be an important step in promoting responsible and ethical use. - Transparency and accountability: It is important to be open and transparent regarding the limitations and pitfalls of models developed with Keras to avoid unintended consequences. Furthermore, accountability can be ensured through initiatives such as auditing and third-party verification of models developed with Keras.

In conclusion, building a thriving open-source ecosystem around Keras requires attention to fostering collaboration, ensuring reproducibility and promoting responsible and ethical use of deep learning technologies. With clear guidelines and policies, access to resources, and collaborative community efforts, we can develop and maintain successful open-source deep learning projects.